Holiness in the everyday

David Cadman

Published 2009 by Quaker Books,
Friends House, 173 Euston Road, London NW1 2BJ
www.quaker.org.uk

ISBN 978 1 907123 04 7

Enquiries should be addressed to Quaker Books, Quaker Communications,
Friends House, 173 Euston Road, London NW1 2BJ

Printed on recycled paper by Information Press Ltd

Britain Yearly Meeting of the Religious Society of Friends (Quakers) is a
registered charity no. 1127633

To Elizabeth, Sophie and Sam

Contents

Acknowledgements

In addition to all those who have been my guide along the way, I would like to thank Ben Pink Dandelion of Woodbrooke for encouraging me to submit these texts for publication, Peter Daniels for his work as copy editor and all those from Quaker Books who have helped. Writing is a solitary practice and the company of others is a great comfort.

Introduction

For everything that lives is Holy.[1]

In recent years, Quakers have been discussing "testimony", the ways in which Quakers express their faith individually and corporately.[2] Part of this concern has arisen in the belief that Quakers are withdrawing too much from the world, perhaps retreating into a private spirituality, perhaps becoming too comfortably middle class, stained by a common culture of individualism, materialism and consumerism. It has also been said that, as a consequence, Quakers have begun to lose the spirit of "dissent" that should always be a part of their testimony.

Because Quakers do not subscribe to a set doctrine or creed, the discussion of testimony is always going to be problematic. And yet there are testimonies – on peace, simplicity, equality and truthfulness – which most Quakers would subscribe to and regard as part of what it means to be a Quaker. Indeed, more recently, most would add the testimony on what some would call "stewardship" and others "sustainability", a testimony that expresses our relationship with the Earth.

---

[1] William Blake, *The Marriage of Heaven and Hell: A Song of Liberty*.
[2] See, for example, Jonathan Dale and others, *Faith in Action: Quaker social testimony*, (2000, repr. 2007).

I am a "birthright" Quaker, and became so familiar in childhood with these testimonies that later in life I think I did not give them proper attention; but my interest was rekindled quite recently by taking part with local Friends in a study group centred around a "toolkit" from the Quaker Peace & Social Witness Testimonies Committee, *Engaging with the Quaker Testimonies*.[3] As we shall see later on, one particular phrase in the papers caught my attention: "holy living". I was also taken by the following words in the Foreword written by the Committee:

> It seems to us that a testimony should spring from a place of love...[4]

Good work and dissent are the most important characteristics of what it is to be a Quaker, difficult and essential parts of our testimony. But it seems to me that there is something else every bit as difficult and every bit as much a part of that testimony. At the heart of Quakerism is a quality and discipline which some refer to as "mystical" – waiting quietly upon God with an open heart or, as George Fox would say, standing in the Light. I am deeply attracted to such a notion, and am inclined towards what I would call a "practical mysticism", but the word "mystical" is so set about by interpretation and misunderstanding that I would make use of the Testimonies Committee's expression, "a place of love".

For most of us leading an "ordinary life", this place is found in what is close at hand – in our relationships with our family, our neighbours, those with whom we work and those whose company we enjoy. It is found in small and sometimes not so small acts of kindness and sacrifice and it must be the

---

[3] Quaker Peace & Social Witness Testimonies Committee, *Engaging with the Quaker Testimonies: a Toolkit*, (2007); hereafter referred to as *Testimonies Toolkit*.
[4] *Testimonies Toolkit*, 4.

foundation for reaching out to others, whether they are nearby or far away. This is the ordinary, everyday and holy life. And I want to suggest that this practice of love, arising necessarily from our Quaker form of prayer and worship, is at least a part of our testimony; and that it may help us to nurture the faith and well-being of a community – including the Quaker community.

Most of us do not lead a life of protest, although we may well support those who do, and join with them from time to time. But all of us live a life defined by the ways in which we relate to each other and to the Earth. We can, we must, live these relationships aright, urgently and all the time. If we do, we may find much good has been done and, at least for some of the time, we will have lived in that place where love is found.

Our testimonies may express how we should live – and perhaps how we believe others should live – but what is the ground upon which they are founded? What lies at the root of our testimonies on peace, simplicity, equality and truthfulness, and what is it that governs our relationship with each other and with the Earth? I believe that the root must be Divine Love; that we have, first, to enter into the presence of the Divine; that for action to be True it must be rooted in such presence and in such Love; that contemplation and reflection are the necessary precursor to True Action; and that through such action we shall return to a better and more grounded contemplation.

I also want to suggest that we must live by what we propose; that just as we are asked if the "seeds of war" lie within our everyday life and within our possessions – "our treasures and the furniture of our houses, and the garments in which we array ourselves"[5] – so too we should ask ourselves if the

---

[5] John Woolman, *A Plea for the Poor*, quoted in Reginald Reynolds, *The Wisdom of John Woolman*, (1948, repr. 1988), 142.

"seeds of peace" lie there. We may need to express ourselves in protest but we should first express ourselves in what we propose, not least through the way we live our daily and ordinary lives – for this is where most of us reside, as indeed do most of our neighbours, however near or far away from us they may be.

In the following essays, I seek to explore this theme through sharing thoughts on holiness, love, simplicity, peace, prayer and that relationship with each other and the Earth we now call "sustainability". Each of these essays is to some extent self-contained, but I hope that together they witness to the need for an intimate relationship between practical action and that deep and disciplined contemplation of the Divine Presence, that turning towards God which I believe lies at the root of Quaker testimony. This is not a plea for a withdrawal from life but a plea for a vital connection between worship, prayer and action.

Chapter 1

On Holiness[1]

> It seems to us that a testimony should spring from
> a place of love rather than fear, have a corporate
> dimension, be about witness as well as coming from
> the divine, and, like an act of worship, lead us back
> to the divine. But the ultimate test of testimony is
> whether Friends live it.[2]

The words we use to describe our daily lives come in time
to shape them. They are never neutral but carry particular
meaning. They shape our lives because they give expression to
our underlying values – to that which we hold to be True.

Sometimes, the dominant culture of a time can so mis-
shape a word that it becomes almost impossible to use it
without causing deep unease. One of them is the word "holy".

For many people, this word is now very uncomfortable. It is
said to carry a sense of piety and separation, as when we say
that someone is "holier than thou", by which we mean they
are overly self-satisfied and judgemental. Many now prefer
the word "spiritual", which they feel can refer to a sense of the
divine without the oppression of any religious authority – but

---

[1] Parts of this text first appeared in *Inspirations* 5 and 6, 2008.
[2] Testimonies Committee Minute 2006, in *Testimonies Toolkit*, 4.

some people apparently find even this word unacceptable.[3] Some overcome their discomfort by using the word "holistic" but, as the American farmer and poet Wendell Berry has said, "People who use the word 'holistic' are too stuck-up to say 'whole' and too sophisticated to say 'holy'."[4]

I know that if we speak of the holy, and speak of it as being part of the everyday, we invite disapproval. Religious people may accuse us of ignorance, and say holiness is something apart from ordinary life and ordinary individuals, while those who shun the religious life may accuse us of a mixture of foolish piety and irrelevance. And yet not to speak of the holy at all is to remove from our lives a dimension of experience, and this leaves us diminished and at a loss. I am not a theological scholar and am reluctant to undertake learned discourse. But my own experience, my dwelling if you like, tells me of another possibility which is: our everyday lives can be – have to be – transformed into that which is holy.

Warren Kenton, who is a scholar, tells me that in the mystical Judaic tradition of the Kabbalah the sacred and the mundane are understood to be at separate levels of consciousness – the former at a higher level than the latter. The sacred is in the world but not of it. Meanwhile, the holy potentiality of the mundane is united with the sacred by a consciousness that has the potential to become aware of a divine "wholeness". This is the teaching of the sages of all time and of all traditions.

I want to bring the word "holy" back to where it belongs – back into our ordinary lives. For, in truth, this is where it belongs. The word is an old word and stems from the same root as "whole", "healthy" and "hallowed". It speaks of a humility and reverence that is no longer common. It also speaks of devotion: the adoration of the heart that opens us to the love of God; what the Bhagavad Gita refers to as "bhakti".

---

[3] George E. Vailant, "Positive Emotions, Spirituality and the Practice of Psychiatry", *Mens Sana Monographs*, Vol. 6(1), Jan-Dec 2008, 49.
[4] Personal conversation, April 2008.

Compared with the turmoil that so often characterises much of modern life, the holy life is more patient, more mindful, more compassionate, more peaceful, simpler and less attached to either things or opinions. And because thoughtfulness requires time, it has a slower pace. A key component of the holy life is, therefore, a state of peace-full-ness. Indeed, it is said that peacefulness is a necessary root condition: inwardly we should be full of peace; and outwardly we should act in peace.[5] This peacefulness suggests being at one with all that is. The Buddhist sage Nagarjuna says:

> In seeing things
> To be or not to be
> Fools fails to see
> A world at ease.[6]

All that follows is an attempt to show the holy in the everyday, to show how in many ways our lives are already holy, and to show holiness as the way of being that arises when we are most truly ourselves. In all of this, my thoughts are shaped by my Quaker background and by being one who loves the teachings of the Buddha.

On many occasions, when the Buddha was asked, "How shall we live?" he replied by teaching the Four Noble Truths – that there is suffering, that craving is its cause, that the cessation of suffering can be found by letting go of craving, and that this is done by following the Eightfold Path. The Path is of right understanding and motivation, right speech, practice and livelihood, and right effort, mindfulness and concentration.

---

[5] I am thinking especially of my conversations with Dadi Janki and Sister Jayanti of the Brahma Kumaris.
[6] Stephen Batchelor, *Verses from the Centre*, (2000), 90.

Living as we do within a materialist and consumerist culture – with identity and reputation linked to all the things we have or aspire to have – the diagnosis that suffering is caused by craving, by wanting to have, is a tough one for most of us. So much of our lives is set about with "having". Indeed, our happiness is meant to be the result of what we have. And yet many of us know, in our hearts, that the teaching of the Buddha is true. Indeed, research undertaken by the New Economics Foundation shows that despite continuing economic growth our index of well-being has not increased for something like forty years.[7]

Another of the great teachings of the Buddha is the teaching of cause and effect in all things: that one thing will always lead to another. And so, in seeking for solutions to what we might call "our present difficulties", particularly the problems of climate change and resource depletion, we should understand that they have not arisen accidentally or randomly but as a direct consequence of our own behaviour. This means that what we do matters; indeed, it means that what we think matters. Since again, as the Buddha has taught, "with our thoughts we make the world."[8] What we hold to be True becomes concrete in the way in which we live our lives, in the conventions of public life and corporate life, in the places we build, and the ways we relate to each other and to that Nature of which we are but a part.

The Quaker *Advices and Queries*[9] urge us to lead a simple life,

---

[7] www.neweconomics.org.uk
[8] The first stanza of *The Dhammapada*.
[9] Quakers in Britain have neither a creed nor priests to govern their lives, but are guided by *Quaker Faith and Practice* (*QFP*), called in its subtitle a "book of Christian discipline", including 42 *Advices and Queries* (*A&Q*)which are also published separately. As the book itself acknowledges, "discipline" is another word that has become unpopular, but the *Advices and Queries* are offered as "...advice and counsel, the encouragement of self-questioning, of hearing each other in humility and love".

a life of moderation in all things. This guiding principle can at times feel rather like a wet blanket, but it is especially good in our present difficulties when so much of the problem has been caused by profligacy and thoughtlessness. The advice Quakers are given is:

> Try to live simply. A simple lifestyle freely chosen is a source of strength. Do not be persuaded into buying what you do not need or cannot afford.

And the query we have to answer is:

> Do you keep yourself informed about the effects of your style of living on the global economy and the environment?[10]

A section of *Quaker Faith and Practice* entitled "Simplicity and Equality" expresses the importance of simplicity:

> The heart of Quaker ethics is summed up in the word 'simplicity'. Simplicity is forgetfulness of self and remembrance of our humble status as waiting servants of God.[11]

In a more recent text and using words with a strong Buddhist undertone, the Testimonies Committee suggest that

> Simplicity also involves peace and sustainability. A simple life takes us away from the greed that is the root of war.[12]

---

[10] *A&Q* 41 (*QFP*, 1.02).
[11] *QFP* 20.27: this comes from the *Faith and Practice* of North Carolina Yearly Meeting (Conservative), 1983.
[12] *Testimonies Toolkit*, 24.

As I mentioned in the Introduction, somewhat to my surprise but certainly to my delight, this text on the matter of "sustainability and the environment" proposes that learning to live sustainably in some way depends upon holiness. Our testimony for living sustainably "should spring from a place of love rather than from fear" and, although we may struggle to describe "sustainability", it might well be characterised by words such as:

> ...care, respect, love, symbiosis, honouring, valuing, hospitality, stewardship, nurture, humility, adaptation and accommodation, peaceable living, interconnectedness, awe, wonder, relationship, harmony, consecration, sacramental or holy living.[13]

While many of us would say "Amen" to that, I suspect most of us would find it difficult to describe how the sacramental or holy life might be lived.[14]

Oddly enough, and given that we seem so often to be confused about this, the teachings of the New Testament are clear. According to the gospels, the overriding commandment is that we should "love one another",[15] that we should be peacemakers, meek, merciful and pure in heart and that we should "turn the other cheek" and "go the extra mile".[16]

Such a selfless way of life can be derided as entirely "unrealistic". And yet whose realism are we talking about? I have found that much of my life has been surrounded by people who live their lives in this way, living by co-operation and compromise, by neighbourliness and a care for each other,

---

[13] *Testimonies Toolkit*, 55.

[14] This next section is based upon an article "Divine Abiding and the holy life" that first appeared in *The Friends Quarterly*, Vol.36 no.3 (July 2008), 28–33, reprinted with the editor's kind permission.

[15] John 13:34.

[16] Matthew 5, The Sermon on the Mount.

by small – and sometimes not so small – acts of kindness and thoughtfulness.

Furthermore, the most successful businesses I have worked with have been characterised more by generosity and loyalty than by selfishness and aggression. I have found that colleagues respond best to encouragement rather than fear, and continually "go the extra mile". Such behaviour – such holy behaviour, as I would call it – is seldom spoken of and, for reasons I have never quite understood, we commonly proclaim a false myth about how our lives in general and business in particular proceed. We portray the "jungle" in which we are all supposed to live as "red in tooth and claw" when, in truth, if it is a jungle it is one that is made up of a delicate set of reciprocal relationships – the survival of the fitting.

The conventional socio-economic model of the Western world has been profligate and damaging to the Earth. However, this damage has been caused as much by a profound misapprehension as by a deliberate selfishness. The priests of our economy – and we as their flock – have had a blind faith in what now looks very much like a false god. At root, the common and fatal systemic flaw underlying present dilemmas such as climate change and the credit crunch may not be an inherent human weakness but rather a particular form of human ignorance.

The Buddhist teaching of reality, of how things come to be as they are – the teaching known as *paticca-samuppāda* or dependent origination[17] – tells us that our circle of suffering arises from three roots: greed, hatred and ignorance. And, counter-wise, that the circle of the end of suffering arises from generosity, loving-kindness and wisdom. Wherever you start from, one thing will certainly follow on from another. So we

---

[17] See, for example, the Preface to *The Long Discourses of the Buddha*, translated by Maurice Walshe, (1995), 34 et seq., or Walpola Rahula, *What the Buddha Taught*, (1974), 53 et seq.

might at least be prepared to agree that it is the *unholy* life that is "unrealistic" for it will in the end be the one that leads to failure. As we can see, greed and hatred appear to have their own inevitable consequences in the degradation of Nature and of our lives.

Certainly greed and ignorance must underlie both climate change and the credit crunch – our rapacious appetite for consumption and financial gain and our inability to see the consequences of our actions. Nothing, surely, could be more emblematic of our present time than the failure of the banking system. On the one hand it purports to represent stability and responsibility and to be the measure of the best of life; on the other hand, in reality, it would seem to represent instability, foolishness and recklessness.

Another of the Buddha's seminal teachings, and one that may help us in the search for holy living, is the teaching of "divine abiding" – the teaching of the Four Sublime States or *brahma-vihāra*. These four states are loving-kindness (*mettā*), compassion (*karunā*), sympathetic joy in others (*muditā*) and equanimity (*upekkhā*).[18] Again, as with the teachings of Jesus, these qualities are often present in our lives, and while they are commonly said to be unworldly or unrealistic, the teachings both of Jesus and of the Buddha challenge this supposition. Indeed, the teaching of the Buddha is that seeing things as they really are can *only* be done by this divine abiding, that without it we will never be able to see this world for what it is. And then, in the parable of the vine, Jesus says something very much akin to this:

> Abide in me, and I in you. As the branch cannot bear fruit of itself, except it abide in the vine; no more can ye, *except* ye abide in me.[19] [my emphasis]

---

[18] See for example, *The Middle Length Discourse of the Buddha*, translated by Bhikkhu Ñānamoli and Bhikkhu Bodhi, (1995), 5 and Suttas 7 and 40.
[19] John 15:4.

In both cases, then, the teaching would seem to be that "the holy life" or "divine abiding" is not some separate practice reserved for monks and nuns but the necessary grounding for all our lives; and not for some part of our lives but for our lives as a whole. Indeed, we should also note that such a life is not in any way alien to us. On the contrary, according to the teachings it is, in the deepest sense, familiar to us, for when we live it we are most our truly ourselves.

If it seems certain we cannot expect to find solutions to our present problems by following the path that has led us to them, might it then be these supposedly unrealistic teachings that must be our guide as we try and extract ourselves from an old and outmoded culture and from an old and outmoded economy based upon a set of deeply embedded but flawed propositions? Is it possible that the qualities and principles inherent in these timeless teachings of Jesus and the Buddha are the very qualities we now need to enable us to find our way out of climatic and economic disruption? I believe so.

But how might this be expressed in practice?

By way of example, let us start with the matter of banking and investment. What we have seen recently – but which has been brewing for some years – is that unholy quality, greed, being raised to a principle that cannot be challenged, expressed in financial mechanisms that have insisted on an ever-growing separation of investment from the raw assets on which in reality its returns depend. Thus we have seen an ever-burgeoning array of financial derivatives, often coupled with significant gearing or borrowing, that appear to offer both liquidity and outstanding returns – for ever! This intoxicating froth, which seemed for a while to offer us ambrosia, was in truth a fantasy, disconnected from and quite unrelated to true worth.

By contrast, the teachings of the holy life are rooted in the notion of connection and relationship. So, when we come to markets, they would ask us to give attention to the quality of the relationships these markets describe, the extent to which prices and financial values are well grounded and, yes, sustainable. For sustainability has as much to do with economy as it has to do with environment

The humble mortgage provides us with an interesting example of this. There was a time when a mortgage company would attract funds from savers and use these savings as the foundation for lending money to house buyers on the collateral of their houses – using, as governing principles, a set of sustainable relationships such as sound liquidity ratios and never lending more than 75% of value or more than two and a half to three times a person's working income. Recognising this reciprocal relationship, these companies were called "mutuals", and principles of "affordability" were deemed important as a test of repayments and thence of the rate of interest payable to savers – a set of dynamic but clearly understood relationships that sought a fair balance, a mutuality, between the needs of both savers and borrowers.

But for some, this was not enough and many such companies were urged to let go of their mutual status and "go public", serving shareholders rather than either savers or borrowers. This required not only "performance" but "improved performance", each and every year. At the same time, by changing a house from a place in which to live into an asset in which to invest, the nature of the relationship between the house owner and the house was changed, and this was further degraded as the value of the house then came to be seen as the collateral for personal expenditure – a fundamental blurring of the distinction between capital and income, with the former falsely being used as a surrogate for the latter.

Such pressures and such changes, based upon what the Buddha would have called greed, were according to his doctrine bound to fail. And they have – not by accident but by consequence: a consequence of the inevitable relationship between what we hold to be true and what we then do, between belief, action and outcomes.

If we were to follow the principles of the holy life, we would have to come back to those qualities set out in the *Testimonies Toolkit*:

> ...care, respect, love, symbiosis, honouring, valuing, hospitality, stewardship, nurture, humility, adaptation and accommodation, peaceable living, interconnectedness, awe, wonder, relationship, harmony, consecration, sacramental or holy living.[20]

If such a set of wholesome or holy principles governed our investment management and behaviour, they would surely have acted as a check to the flagrant greed and opportunism of the now sorrowful banks and building societies. For they forgot what they used to know and thereby became un-wholesome, which is to say, un-holy. By following wholesome or holy principles, by being stewards of the basic relationship between savers and borrowers, it would surely have been possible to continue providing funds for people to buy houses and, as it happens, to do so in a manner that would probably have dampened the rise in house prices, thereby making buying a house – a house to live in rather than a house as an investment – more rather than less affordable.

Perhaps, by default, we shall return to such ways, since savers are likely to transfer their funds away from the profligate banks and towards the old mutuals, favouring their more humble aspirations. If this is so, perhaps it might give us time to rethink the true purpose of our banks and building societies, and how they might be governed and managed in accordance with those principles of connectedness and stewardship described by the holy life.

---

[20] *Testimonies Toolkit*, 55.

The unholy economic profligacy, selfishness and myopia that have led to global warming and climate change are a similar expression of a fatal disconnectedness or unrelatedness in economic behaviour. A form of what the Buddha would no doubt have called ignorance.

However, we are now beginning to understand that our lives and our ways of being are deeply interconnected. A part of this is understanding – or at least becoming aware of – the dynamic relationships between the economy, society and the environment. Amidst all the evidence of possible catastrophe (which I do not in the least discount), there are grounds for hope as we, as individuals, families, communities, businesses, and belatedly as nations, appear to accept the need for a significant shift of perception – a move from an old world and an old economy to a new world and a new economy, a move towards a more wholesome and, I would say, holy way of living.

In my own work, I have seen a quite extraordinary shift in the expectations and aspirations of young people coming into work and requiring that their employer demonstrate what is sometimes called "responsibility" but might be called stewardship. I have seen an investment community develop responsible policies, and put considerable sums of money into becoming informed of the changes needed to adapt to and mitigate climate change. I have seen individuals, businesses and communities tackle not only the daily good practice of such things as energy efficiency and recycling but also the more fundamental changes in perception, policy and action that they now accept as a necessary calling-in of the debt of their own profligacy.

Behind all of this is a structural shift towards a set of timeless principles of wholesomeness, stewardship and interconnectedness which might be said to represent holy living or a divine abiding. That which is holy unites while that which is unholy separates and divides. To bear fruit, the branch must abide in the vine. Divine abiding requires that we care for others with loving-kindness, compassion and joy in their happiness. It also requires that we practice discernment and equanimity. This is where we must all come to. In a world of frenetic activity, we have to understand and profess the importance of reflection as the root of true action. That a holy life must be sustained by daily prayer and blessed silence. That living sustainably "should spring from a place of love rather than from fear".[21]

As I have said, to use the word "holy" in our time is either an act of bravery or foolishness, for there will be many who will say that such a word is "out of time". But the word is timeless and in many ways also ordinary, a part of our common remembrance. All of the great spiritual traditions tell us that the holy life springs from Divine Love and is found in peacefulness, discipline and generosity. These three qualities are seen to be in contrast to hatred, disorder and greed. They are qualities that arise from a concern for others in contrast to an obsession with one's self.

And where should we start? That, too, is easy, since all these great spiritual traditions make it clear that outward peace and well-being cannot be achieved without inner peace and well-being. We start with ourselves.

We may sometimes feel that the small things we do to simplify our lives and reduce our carbon footprint – improving the insulation of our houses, buying our electricity on a green tariff, recycling, travelling less, buying local food and catching the rain from our gutters in a water butt – is as nothing compared with the number of coal-fired power stations being built in China or another ludicrous hotel complex in Dubai, but remember that this *is* where we have to start. Perhaps we will also be able to influence things more widely but only if we *start here*, with ourselves and with what

---

[21] *Testimonies Toolkit*, 4.

is close at hand. For without this, it is all words and opinions, and how can we expect others to change their lives unless we are prepared to change our own? In this, those Quaker words may turn out to be a useful guide:

> ...care, respect, love, symbiosis, honouring, valuing, hospitality, stewardship, nurture, humility, adaptation and accommodation, peaceable living, interconnectedness, awe, wonder, relationship, harmony, consecration, [and, of course] sacramental or holy living.[22]

...at least to start with!

---

[22] *Testimonies Toolkit*, 55.

Chapter 2

On Love

Take heed, dear Friends, to the promptings of love
and truth in your hearts. Trust them as the leadings of
God...[1]

At the root of holiness is Love.

In a world of shift and change, I suppose each one of us
sometimes wonders how it is we have come to be where we
are, what it is that has shaped our lives and what has been
our true purpose.[2] For most of the time, our lives seem to be
determined by a never-ending sequence of quite mundane
duties and tasks: schooling and college, work and family, the
usual trials and tribulations of life. Furthermore, at least in
the West, there is a strong presumption that even though
time may pass we must stay forever young, that old age is to
be avoided and, indeed, feared. By contrast, in the traditions
of India there is a wiser perspective governing the passing
of the years. The first parts of life are the life as student and
then as householder, busy times in which we are very much

---

[1] *Advices and Queries*, 1 (*QFP*, 1.02.1).
[2] This next section is taken as an extract from my contribution to a
felicitation for Prof. Suheil Bushrui, *The Value of Values*, edited by
Mehrdad Nassoudi, (U. of Maryland 2005), parts of which were used
in a lecture to the New York School of Design in April 2008.

engaged with the external world of affairs and responsibilities. But it is recognised that there will come a time when we should lay down these tasks and turn inwards, not – at least at first – to renounce the world but to engage with it in quite a different way; a time in which the pace of life slows down, we become more inclined to dwell in one place and are more contemplative and reflective.

The following passage from the *Discourses of the Buddha* clearly takes us to the same place, the place where we begin to let go of "the world's bait":

Life is swept along, short is the life span;
No shelters exist for one who has reached old age.
Seeing clearly this danger in death,
A seeker of peace should drop the world's bait.

Time flies by, the nights swiftly pass;
The stages of life successively desert us.
Seeing clearly this danger in death,
A seeker of peace should drop the world's bait.[3]

This is where I find myself. And, looking back, I see that there have been two vital influences shaping my life and bringing me to this place. The first is an inheritance of Quakerism with its blessed silence and the words and parables of Jesus. The second, later, is the teaching of the Buddha. I understand people who say you must choose a path and stick to it, but in my case these two paths have become intertwined like a honeysuckle and a rose. The rose is my birthright and was in place before the honeysuckle, the teaching of the Buddha, grew upon it. Now their fragrance has become one. For they are rooted together, grounded in love and compassion.

---

[3] *The Connected Discourses of the Buddha*, translated by Bhikkhu Bodhi, (2000), 90–91.

One morning some while ago, sitting in the stillness of a Quaker meeting, I felt myself overcome by a deep gloom. As usual that morning, I had turned on my radio to hear the news and was dealt a dose of "the war on terrorism", "the axis of evil" and other such matters. This storm of words had hovered over my head and now it settled there like a dark cloud. I suppose what made it so dark was the way it was assumed that the only way to tackle these matters was by armed conflict, by attacking the outward manifestation of all of this hate and sorrow. And what made it worse was that I really could not think of an alternative.

And then a Friend rose to speak. At first I have to confess that my mind was elsewhere but then a shiver went down my spine as I heard the words: "Let us then try what Love will do..." At that moment, these words from William Penn struck my heart as both profoundly simple and profoundly radical. This is the quotation in a fuller form:

> A good end cannot sanctify evil means; nor must we ever do evil that good may come of it... We are too ready to retaliate, rather than forgive or gain by love and information. And yet we could hurt no man that we believe loves us. Let us then try what Love will do: for if men did once see we love them, we should soon find they would not harm us. Force may subdue, but Love gains: and he that forgives first, wins the laurel.[4]

It seemed to me then, and it seems to me now, that if we are required to find a new pathway to confront the perils of the twenty-first century, we might follow this simple but radical proposition: "Let us then try what Love will do".

I recognise at once that to speak of Love is fraught with

---

[4] William Penn, *Some Fruits of Solitude*, (1978), maxims 537, 543–546; also in *QFP* 24.03.

difficulty and misunderstanding. "Love" as a word has become so used, and misused, that it might be supposed that I am speaking of mere sentimentality or, indeed, of the passions of the body. But I am not. I am trying to speak of something rather different, something at one and the same time both more common and more profound than either of these. For what I want to suggest is this: Love is the very foundation of reality – that which *is*, is Love.

This is what is captured in the Arabic word "Mahabbah", which means Love as the underlying principle of the universe.[5] It is the very "breath of Divinity". In the words of the American philosopher, Whittal N. Perry:

> Love is the energizing elixir of the universe, the cause and effect of all harmonies, light's brilliance and the heat in wine and fire, it is the aroma of perfumes and the breath of the Divinity: it is the Life in all being... It is all that the texts have to say, and the more that remains unspoken.[6]

It is what the Christian mystic Julian of Norwich refers to as "our Lord's meaning":

> From time to time these things were first revealed. I had often wanted to know what was our Lord's meaning. It was more than fifteen years after that I was answered in my spirit's understanding. "You would know our Lord's meaning in this thing? Know it well. Love was his meaning. Who showed it you? Love. What did he show you? Love. Why did he show it? For love. Hold on to this and you will know and understand

---

[5] I am most grateful to Professor Suheil Bushrui for pointing this out to me. The word is part of the teaching of the Bahá'ís.
[6] Whitall N. Perry, *A Treasury of Traditional Wisdom*, (2000), 612.

love more and more. But you will not know or learn anything else – ever!" So it was that I learned that love was our Lord's meaning." [7]

In the teachings of Jesus, the vital importance of Love as an informing principle is self-evident:

Master [he was asked], which is the greatest commandment in the law?
Jesus said unto him, Thou shalt love the Lord thy God with all thy heart, and with all thy soul, and with all thy mind.
This is the first and great commandment.
And the second is like unto it, Thou shalt love thy neighbour as thyself.
On these two commandments hang all the law and the prophets.[8]

And again:

This is my commandment, That ye love one another, as I have loved you.[9]

These teachings are so familiar that we may not quite hear what is being said; we may fail to understand the real profundity. It seems to me the teaching is not simply that love is a virtue (which, of course, it is) or an emotion (which, of course, it is) but that it is *of the essence*. Indeed, in the first epistle of John, it is stated with the utmost directness. Here it is taught, in words as simple as they are profound, that

---

7 *Julian of Norwich: Revelations of Divine Love.* Translated by Clifton Wolters, Penguin Books, (1966) 211–212.
8 Matthew 23:36–40
9 John 15:12.

God is love.[10]

The great mystery that has no name, the divine presence, the One, the All, *is Love*. And if God is in all things then Love is in all things. In the words of the gospel of Thomas, everywhere is where God is:

I am the All
The All comes forth from me,
And the All reaches towards me.
Cleave the wood, I am there;
lift the stone,
and you shall find me there.[11]

And so where we find God we must find Love. This is a most radical proposition. For if Love *is* of the essence, if Love *is* in all, if Love *defines* Truth and Reality, then we would be most unwise to live our lives other than in accordance with its principles.

The teachings of the Buddha take us to the same place. Of course, the Buddha did not claim to be divine nor did he teach of a divine being or God. He did, however, teach that each of the *brahma-vihāra*, the Four Sublime States, the Divine Abodes,[12] is an expression of Love: loving-kindness, compassion, joy in others and equanimity. By dwelling within these subtle expressions of Love, we dwell not in delusion but in Reality, we are one with the essence of all that truly is. Indeed, it is only by so dwelling that we can see things as they really are.[13]

---

[10] I John 4:8.
[11] *The Gospel of Thomas*, presented by Hugh McGregor Ross, (1987), logion 77
[12] In Pali, the four divine abodes are the *brahma-vihāra*, which are *mettā* (loving-kindness), *karunā*, (compassion), *muditā* (appreciative joy) and *upekkhā* (equanimity).
[13] *The Middle Length Discourses of the Buddha*, translated by Bhikkhu Ñānamoli and Bhikkhu Bodhi, (1995), Sutta 52, the *Atthakanāgara Sutta*.

At the centre of this is the Buddha's teaching on loving-kindness, the *Metta Sutta*, which is clear as to practice:

This is what should be done
By those who are skilled in goodness,
And who know the path of peace:
Let them be able and upright,
Straightforward and gentle in speech.
Humble and not conceited,
Contented and easily satisfied.
Unburdened with duties, and frugal in their ways.
Peaceful and calm, and wise and skilful,
Not proud and demanding in nature.
Let them not do the slightest thing
That the wise would later reprove.
Wishing: in gladness and in safety,
May all beings be at ease.
Whatever living beings there may be;
Whether they are weak or strong, omitting none,
The great or the mighty, medium, short or small,
The seen and the unseen,
Those living near and far away,
Those born and to-be-born –
May all beings be at ease!
Let none deceive another,
Or despise any being in any state.
Let none through anger or ill-will
Wish harm upon another.
Even as a mother protects with her life
Her child, her only child,
So with a boundless heart
Should one cherish all living beings;
Radiating kindness over the entire world:
Spreading upwards to the skies,
And downwards to the depths;

Outward and unbounded,
Freed from hatred and ill-will.
Whether standing or walking, seated or lying down,
Free from drowsiness,
One should sustain this recollection.
This is said to be the sublime abiding.
By not holding fixed views,
The pure hearted one, having clarity of vision,
Being freed from all sense desires,
Is not born again into this world.[14]

In this teaching, in his teachings of the Four Noble Truths
and in the vital teachings of *paticcasamuppāda* or dependent
origination, the Buddha offered a profound glimpse of the
true nature of Reality, a reality which is dependent upon
the characteristics of Love. For, as he made clear in these
teachings, "that which is" can only be found in that which is in
a state of relatedness. This is a teaching of interconnectedness,
a teaching of relationships made manifest by causation and
consequence:

When this is, that is.
This arising, that arises.
When this is not that is not.
This ceasing, that ceases.[15]

Nothing is separate and absolute. Reality is characterised by
relationship, and all is drawn together by a web of causality
that binds one thing to another, one event to another, one
person to another and to all that is: and what binds is Love. If
we explore this "reality of relatedness", if we open our hearts
and dwell within it, we find it is in fact no more nor less than

---

[14] This translation of the *Metta Sutta*, itself a part of the *Sutta Nipāta*, is
from Sharon Salzberg, *Lovingkindness*, (1995).
[15] Walpola Rahula, *What the Buddha Taught*, (1974), 53; AN X.92.

a profound and mysterious form of Love. For what is Love if it is not that which binds us together, and gives expression to the mystery of arising and ceasing, the turn of the seasons and of our lives, one with another? We are so unused to expecting this, that we may fail to see the expression of Love in all that is around us.

As the Dalai Lama put it at a talk in London in 2004,[16] surely at birth the baby and the mother are drawn together in a vital relationship of Love; and surely, also, at death many of us will be surrounded by those that love us. In this way, Love is natural; it pervades all that is. If we are blessed, Love is there at our beginning and at our end.

To return to my proposition: what we are talking about here is not something that is simply desirable (although, of course, it is) but something that is "of the essence".

But for us there is a difficulty. We have so lost a sense of the sacred that the word "love" has been diminished; has, perhaps, come to mean little more than personal desire, affection or even sentimentality. In truth, love (perhaps with a capital "L") is something much more profound; it is of the nature of True Being – a divine abiding.

What then can be said of this "divine abiding"? At the heart of my Quaker childhood, with its emphasis upon silent contemplation, nonviolence and tolerance, was a teaching that stressed the strength and gentleness of Christ the "good shepherd" – his compassion for the suffering of others and his assurance that the kingdom of heaven would not be found by the rich and the powerful but by the meek, the merciful and the pure in heart. I was brought up to believe in "turning the other cheek" and in the parable of the Good Samaritan. Jesus was a man who taught kindliness and selflessness and, of course, who encapsulated the core of his teaching in the following words:

---

[16] The Temenos Singhvi Lecture, London, 28 May 2004.

A new commandment I give unto you, That ye love one another; as I have loved you, that ye also love one another.[17]

Many years later, it seems to me that this teaching is even more profound than I had supposed. Not only are we being taught that we should love one another as a matter of virtue; we are, I believe, being taught that Love is of the essence – it is "of God", by which I mean "of all that is". For it is also said:

We are of God... for love is of God... God is love; and he that dwelleth in love dwelleth in God, and God in him... because as he is, so are we in this world. [18]

If, then, Love is True, what kind of a reality does it reveal? And if we are to live in the Reality of Love, what are the principles that should govern our lives? Fortunately, the answers to these questions are readily available. We may find the teachings of Jesus and of the Buddha difficult to accept, drenched as we are in Western materialism and cynicism, but they are as clear as could be. They are the teaching of holiness.

The Christian teaching on the characteristics of Love is so well known that, again, we may not realise its profundity. Paul's First Letter to the Corinthians[19] describes the characteristics of Love and the text is so especially beautiful that I cannot resist quoting it in full:

Love suffereth long, and is kind; love envieth not; love vaunteth not itself, is not puffed up,

---

[17] John 13:34.
[18] I John 4: 6–17.
[19] I Corinthians 13.

Doth not behave itself unseemly, seeketh not her own,
    is not easily provoked, Thinketh no evil;
Rejoiceth not in iniquity, but rejoiceth in the truth;
Beareth all things, believeth all things, hopeth all
    things, endureth all things.
Love never faileth

Equally beautiful and clear are the Ten Perfections or
paramitas of the Buddha. They are:

Generosity, morality, renunciation, wisdom, energy,
patience, truthfulness, resolution, loving-kindness and
equanimity.[20]

Furthermore, we find that Love is not desire or possession; it
is desirelessness and non-attachment, a surrendering of one's
self. It is not having but being.

And if this sounds "unrealistic", what does that say of our
so-called "realism"? Having pursued *our* version of reality
what do we see when we look about us? Do we not see a
world profoundly out of order, an environment degraded and
polluted? Is there not much evidence to suggest that our ways
of life, stripped of any sense of the sacred, are dangerously
raising us up against Nature? And, when we look within our
hearts, do we not find something profoundly troubling about
this, about a reality which denies those qualities that alone
can lead us from our basest to our highest being?

Surely, even to the most materialistic and cynical of us,
there is ample evidence of a direct relationship between the
degradation of our selves and the degradation of Nature.
This was certainly the proposition of a rather extraordinary
and remarkable twentieth century German scientist, Viktor
Schauberger, who, as far back as the 1950s, in his study of the

---

[20] Nyanatikola, *Buddhist Dictionary*, (1997), 147–8.

hidden workings of Nature, predicted our present climatic disturbance when he proposed that

> modern human culture's destruction of the creative energies of Nature would result in greater violence and depravity in society. [21]

Indeed, he suggested that if we wanted to see a reversal of this observable deterioration of human society, and a gradual coming back into balance of a humanity which would enable us to live in tune with Nature, we would have to "heed what Nature requires of us".[22] How different this is from a convention that seeks to exploit Nature and turn her to our needs, to make her serve our ends.

Why is it that we act in this harmful way? Perhaps we do so because we are somehow prevented from seeing the Truth. For so much of what we take to be "real" is distorted by the glass through which we are persuaded to look. For example, we are asked to believe in competition as the driving force of life, of the "selfish gene" and the supposedly benign but distant influence of the "hidden hand" of the uncontrolled market place. And yet, in nearly forty years of working in the world of business and commerce, I have found that what really makes a company successful is not so much competition as co-operation. In professional life, many of us have not only spent endless hours developing deep relationships of trust between ourselves and our clients but have also spent time developing networks of friendship and trust among our fellow professionals. Despite the recent influence of a narrow concern for rights and litigation, we have learnt that without these relationships and mutual responsibilities, business is almost impossible to transact; indeed, we discover that these very

---

[21] *The Schauberger Keys*, 18.
[22] see also Alick Bartholomew, *Hidden Nature: The Startling Insights of Viktor Schauberger*, Floris Books, (2003).

relationships of reciprocity are what enable business to be done effectively and well.

Here in the UK, there is a tradition of responsible ownership. It has been put under some stress by more recent intrusive notions of greed and selfishness, but this spirit remains engrained in our culture. Whatever its shortcomings, the recent rise of what is termed "corporate responsibility" in the UK is an example of this. Many people, especially looking in from the outside, mock this new concern as being no more than a cynical and superficial manipulation of information – something that is no more than skin deep. But my own experience of working with companies, first on environmental management and then on sustainability and corporate responsibility, leads me to another conclusion. Yes, there is evidence of a small minority wanting to use this new concern cynically, but many more have begun to understand the connection between their economic aims and their environmental and social impacts. They can see in fact that no economic activity takes place except within some environmental and social context. Because of this, they want to manage these relationships well. Furthermore, they feel comfortable with the challenge this presents, and despite their occasional complaints (or more often the complaints of those purporting to represent them), they are committed to the recognition that this is a new reality – not a fad, not mere compliance, but acceptance of a new "licence to operate".

The ways we work with each other, and the ways companies are coming to understand their relationships with the environment and with society, are *in essence* expressions of this "reality of Love", an unconscious expression of an innate holiness. They are founded upon a growing understanding of the relatedness of our lives. And if, as I have suggested, Love is of the essence, why would this not be so? If Love is in all that *is*, whether we know it or not, it is in all that we *do*. It is at the root of all those things that help us to work together, all those ways in which, every day and without thought, we trust each other – ways that are in my experience more present and durable than their opposites, the denial of community and trust, which in their darkest forms leads to violence and hatred.

In answer to the question "Who is my neighbour?", Jesus taught of this need to care for each other in the parable of the Samaritan. And the Buddha understood that violence and hatred are, in fact, the actions of the ignorant, actions which will inevitably lead to suffering and the repetition of suffering.

The real concern, then, is our ignorance. The concern is that despite (or perhaps because of) our undoubted sophistication and technical brilliance, we fail see things as they really are; we do not, cannot, see that our supposed reality is actually false. We dwell in ignorance – the very condition that is the foundation of suffering. So it is not in the least surprising to find we are unable to see the Truth – the Truth that is staring us in the face. The Truth is there to be read in the book of Nature but in our ignorance we do not, cannot, see it. In the face of co-operation, we see only competition; in the face of oneness, we see only separation; in the face of community we see only hostility. And the more we follow this path, the more difficult it is to see the Truth. As a consequence, we have lost our way, we have become *dis*-eased, *un*-balanced and *dis*-harmonious.

It was part of Viktor Schauberger's work to point to this imbalance in our lives. According to him, Nature is made up of polarities – hot and cold, positive energy and negative energy and so on. To be healthy, said Schauberger, Nature requires a vital balance of the polarities and one that rather favours the negative/feminine over the positive/masculine, the *yin* over the *yang*.[23] Indeed, our imbalance has come about because

---

[23] *The Schauberger Keys*, 15.

we have overstated the latter against the former. We have favoured the expansive, egoistic, rationalistic qualities of the male against the inclusive, intuitive, compassionate qualities of the female.

To restore our balance, we have to allow these feminine characteristics to have greater influence in all we do, and it is interesting to note that the feminine qualities are the ones closest to Paul's definition of Love and the Buddha's *paramitas* or perfections. We need to reorder the balance between the expansive and the integrative, the individual and the community, between quantity and quality and, in contrast to our present culture, we should favour the integrative, the communal and the qualitative. For Love is that which makes whole; that which integrates; that which heals.

But how can this re-ordering be done? Is it really possible for us to make this kind of change? Perhaps.

According to the good and wise Buddha, "our life is the creation of our mind":[24] with our thoughts we make the world. And so, on this analysis, what is now needed is no less than a change of mind, a *metanoia*.

Another way to say this is to say that what we believe in matters. And it matters because, whatever it is, it will shape our lives. We will become what we believe in, for what we look for is nearly always what we find. We have, therefore, to look at *that which we hold to be true*. When all else is stripped away, what is it that defines who we are; and, most importantly, what is it that governs our way of being?

There are, perhaps, two visions of the world that have come to shape our lives at the beginning of the twenty-first century – and both are essentially materialistic. The first is

---

[24] The opening stanza of the *Dhammapada*.

the vision of what is commonly called "mechanistic science" and the second is the vision of what is commonly called "the workings of the market place". Although both of these visions on their own are now somewhat outmoded, their influence persists, and it persists in describing a world made up of separate parts.

Whether we are describing a physical system or a market place – or indeed anything else – we have been encouraged to believe that the way it works is something like a clock, whose workings can best be understood by dismantling it and studying its parts – whether cogs and wheels, atoms and molecules, buyers and sellers, or whatever else. Most importantly, both these powerful but now outmoded visions – mechanistic science and the workings of the market place – suppose that whatever is real, and of real value, is *only* whatever can be measured or priced. Conversely, they imply that whatever is not readily measured or priced is in some sense unreal and of no value.

Thus, according to these visions (or, as I would call them, heresies), "the real world" is confined to that which is tangible, concrete and fixed. Furthermore, it is not only confined to those things that can be measured but also, and most especially, to those things that can be possessed and consumed. And the real dilemma is that this way of seeing the world – useful and productive in its own way but nevertheless limited in its relevance – has come to be taken as having universal application. It is applied not simply to some kinds of science and to some kinds of market transaction but to all we do. It has come to define and limit our experience. It is everywhere and governs all. It has brought us to where we are, and if we would rather be somewhere else we had best find a new vision.

The scholar Joseph Milne explains this well when he talks of three different "languages", three different modes of thought – the empirical, the philosophical and the religious. Each of these has its place but the difficulty arises when either one is used to the exclusion of the others or they are thoughtlessly mixed together. For example, whilst the empirical language of physics can tell us wonderful things, it cannot enter into the realm of metaphysics, the realm of meaning and being. "God" cannot be the object of either empirical or philosophical enquiry, nor will the cure for the common cold be found in the discourse of religion.[25]

Fortunately, although according to convention there are no realities other than those that can be described empirically, there are other visions for us to consider. And one set of such visions, often called the perennial philosophy, has found a voice in all of the great spiritual traditions – whether they be Islam or Christianity or Judaism or Hinduism or Buddhism.

By contrast to the now outmoded atomistic model of "reality" from science and economics, this set of visions offers us a different reality, one that we must call a Divine Reality – characterised most especially by being concerned not with parts but with wholes, not with separateness but with relationship.

These visions tell us that to be whole – indeed, to be real – we have to be at one with what is both within and yet beyond us. We cannot separate ourselves entirely from all that is. Rather we have to practise to become *at one with another* – and this means not only all of humankind but also all beings, all fauna and flora, the mountains and the oceans, the clouds and the winds and the rains.

And if, perhaps in some mysterious way we cannot explain, we are able to see ourselves as an expression of that which is Divine, then reverence for others now present and yet to come must cause us to temper our own desires with those qualities that are the teaching of all the great spiritual traditions – generosity, patience, simplicity, humility, harmlessness, compassion and so on, the very qualities of holiness.

---

[25] Joseph Milne, *Metaphysics and the Cosmic Order*, (2008), 2.

In any event, it seems to me beyond doubt that the vision we choose to guide us will direct our path. If we choose to accept the teachings of convention – materialism and consumerism – we will continue to promote those fantasies promising ever-increasing consumption for all. This will reinforce the environmental and social catastrophes that have already begun to take place – not least flood, famine, pestilence, violence and the resulting economic and political migration – while we continue to wait for the technological and political "fix" that will redeem all. There is, of course, a formidable risk in taking this path but, rather worryingly, it would seem that it *is* the path Western governments are set to follow.

I once heard this story, which tells an important truth. There was a king who failed to live by compassion and to give to the poor. Poor people became poorer. Poverty led to theft, theft to violence and so on and so on until at the lowest point, at the depth of degradation, when all seemed lost, a fool, or so he seemed to others, had the insight and courage to persuade the king to turn away from this seemingly unstoppable tragedy and, once more, proclaim the ancient wisdom of generosity, simplicity and compassion. As he fed the poor, there was less theft; as there was less theft, there was less violence; and so on and so on until, at last, the well-being of all was restored.

Will there now be those "foolish" men and women with the insight and courage to prick the bubble of *our* illusion and turn *us* away from such a calamity? We must pray that this is so.

Fortunately, despite this rather gloomy prognosis, it seems to me that provided we turn to it with resolve and without delay, the second pathway – the path of reverence and sufficiency offered by the perennial philosophy – does at least provide us with the possibility of a more sustainable way.

As I suggest in chapter 3, it is likely that the doctrine of sufficiency and simplicity, today often portrayed as no more than a comfortable alternative for those who already have enough, will in our children's or our grandchildren's time become not an alternative but *a necessity for survival*. For in a quite practical sense it is beyond doubt that although our global trade professes the contrary, this planet cannot support *for all* the level of consumption presently enjoyed by *the few*. For example, we are told that if the people of China were to reach the same level of consumption as those of us in the West (and why should they not want to?), they would absorb in any one year the entire world fish catch, the entire US grain harvest and well in excess of the entire world oil production.[26] And yet such an aspiration not only exists but is being actively promoted, within China and by countries trading there. That means us.

It seems clear, therefore, that in time – and not too distant a time – we must take a different path. We must challenge the conventional definition of reality, abandoning our unbounded materialism and consumption before it is too late and returning once more to the teachings and practice of the great spiritual traditions – the "Divine Reality" of the perennial philosophy.

Finally, I would like to explore just one more part of this pathway. So far, we have been talking about a philosophy, the perennial philosophy. But, on reflection, and particularly for our time, I feel myself drawn towards another phrase, not philosophy but what is called the *sophia eternis*, the "eternal wisdom". For whereas I think that, for us, *philosophy* now speaks of the head, *wisdom* carries with it the promptings of the heart.

As it happens, "philosophy" does, of course, mean the "love of wisdom". I have no doubt that it is Sophia, the goddess of wisdom, who leads us along this pathway of Love, the understanding that Love *is*, which is to say that Love is of

---

26 Lester R. Brown, *Eco-Economy*, (2001).

the essence of being. If we wish to find the Truth, we need to follow this path, for Love is both the pathway and that to which the path will lead us. It is the Quest and the Grail.

Indeed, as Christ taught us, in the end Love is the ground of reality, the still point of being. This being so, we need profoundly to change our perspective, our way of being – to move away from an ethos of separation, conflict and competition towards one of wholeness, co-operation and compassion. Perhaps we can "take heed" of those "promptings of love and truth" to which we, as Quakers, are urged.

Chapter 3

A Necessary Simplicity[1]

Try to live simply. A simple lifestyle freely chosen is a source of strength.[2]

Some while ago, I was asked to review a book called *Timeless Simplicity*,[3] which provided an introduction to the history of simplicity and gave practical guidance as to how it might be lived today. However, as I wrote the review it seemed to me possible that we might take "simplicity" to be just another form of "lifestyle", something available to those who already have enough; that it might be just another "product" to be acquired and possessed. Certainly the colour supplements and glossy magazines are not beyond presenting pictures of an idyllic "simple" life, complete with wellington boots, hybrid 4x4s and beautifully photographed organic vegetables and home made jam – all to be purchased at a price.

It would be reassuring to think that, without too much effort, we could buy our way into "simplicity", having to make only minor adjustments to our present untrammelled ways of life, and that this would save us from all those prophesies

---

[1] This text first appeared in *Resurgence*, no. 217, March/April 2003.
[2] *Advices and Queries* 41, *QFP* 1.02.41.
[3] John Lane, *Timeless Simplicity*, (2001).

of ecological doom. But somehow or other this does not ring true. The uncomfortable truth is that the underlying ethos of our present lives is not just mildly awry but fatally flawed.

The present rationale is that the common good is best achieved through economic growth and prosperity based upon an ever-increasing consumption of products and services. Since it represents convention, the foundation of this rationale is seldom discussed, but one must suppose it to be that human happiness is best attained through satisfying material needs. In fact, if one probes a little deeper it becomes clear that this foundation is not quite as stated. Indeed, the doctrine of consumption and economic growth is *not* primarily founded upon "satisfaction" but upon "*dis*satisfaction". For the system to work it is essential to have the *promise* of satisfaction, but that promise must never be fulfilled. The promise is a lie and is intended to be so – although we are not supposed to notice.

It is rather unsettling, but not surprising, to discover that this deliberately misleading promise was developed in America in the 1920s out of techniques of war-time propaganda, techniques originally used to persuade a reluctant populace to support the war effort. Edward Bernays was very much involved in the First World War propaganda exercise, and afterwards adapted these techniques for commercial and political purposes. His quite deliberate aim was to shape the desires of the American people as part of a new consumerism, allied to an associated political agenda of "keeping the voters happy"[4]. He understood something rather important, which is that the appetite of our present materialism *depends upon* stirring up our wants – but not satisfying them.

---

[4] His book *Propaganda* (1928) begins: "The conscious and intelligent manipulation of the organized habits and opinions of the masses is an important element in democratic society." Full text is online at: www. historyisaweapon.org/defcon1/bernprop.html

This doctrine is reinforced in a more recent observation, again from America:

> Although it is said that the function of the market is to satisfy human wants and so to maximise various satisfactions, it is not true that the function of advertising is to maximise satisfaction; rather its function is to increase people's dissatisfaction with any current state of affairs, to create wants, and to exploit the dissatisfactions of the present. Advertising must use dissatisfaction to achieve its purpose.[5]

Leaving aside the slight sense of repugnance one feels on reading this, the real difficulty is of course that such a system is quite literally unsustainable. We – the peoples of the Earth – do not have the resources needed to continue meeting an ever-growing demand to consume. Nor do we have the capacity to absorb the consequential waste without causing irreversible harm and putting at risk our own lives and the lives of others, not least the lives of plants and animals. And yet the evident dangers of our continuing excess are largely ignored. Indeed, we continue to be urged to increase the volume of our consumption as *the only* recipe for sustaining our well-being. In the face of resource depletion and global warming, what kind of madness is that?

The real danger we face is that if we continue following such a path we will in time, and perhaps not a very distant time, meet catastrophe. There are those who regard such prophecies as overly gloomy. Others point to the growing evidence of catastrophe as natural systems appear to display worrying signs of disturbance and degradation. In any event, if these prophecies are even half correct, change will be imposed upon us. So our real challenge is not that we might *choose* to

---

[5] Robert E Lane, *The Loss of Happiness in Market Democracies*, (2000), 179.

change our ways but that we will *have* to do so – and if this is so, "simplicity" will not be a comfortable option but a *vital necessity*.

This poses another dilemma, for as we systematically colonise so-called "under-developed" societies, bringing Coca-Cola and McDonalds to places that for centuries have been self-sufficient without them, we simultaneously destroy the knowledge of living within one's means – of living simply. In her book *Ancient Futures: Learning from Ladakh*, Helena Norberg-Hodge chronicles not only the costs of such "development" on a society that for centuries has lived in a state of ecological balance and social harmony, but also the lessons that such a "simple" and resourceful society can offer to us, the supposedly "over-developed". This is what she says:

> In Ladakh I have known a society in which there is neither waste nor pollution, a society in which crime is virtually non-existent, communities are healthy and strong, and a teenage boy is never embarrassed to be gentle and affectionate with his mother or grandmother. As that society begins to break down under the pressures of modernization, the lessons are of relevance far beyond Ladakh itself.[6]

And in case the word "simple" is taken to mean impoverished, the lesson of Ladakh is quite the contrary. Here are a people with a rich and satisfying culture, with music, song and story that give meaning and identity to their community. It is our way of life and not theirs that threatens its destruction. Indeed, it is evident that it is our greed and not their simplicity that gives rise to poverty, not least as a consequence of the increasing gap between those with most

---

[6] Helena Norberg-Hodge, *Ancient Futures: Learning from Ladakh*, (1992 and revised edition 2000), 4.

and those with least, and by the loss of diversity and local identity that results from the life-sapping monoculture of globalisation.

So where can we turn to for the guidance we need to find a more sustainable path? Fortunately, despite the awesome and potentially destructive power of our consumerism, there is a long and ever-present tradition of wisdom that awaits our attention. Every culture, and not least our own, has a treasury of stories and myths that tell of the ways to live in harmony with the land. In Britain, such stories are part of the Celtic Mabinogion and of Arthur and the Grail Quest. There are the stories of the Native Americans and the "songlines" of the Aboriginal Australians. Most especially, such teaching lies at the heart of the great spiritual traditions. Take, for example, the lessons of sufficiency of the Jains, the Middle Way of Buddhism and the teachings of selflessness given to us by Christ and by Christian saints such as Francis of Assisi. In all of this there is a code which can lead us along the path of simplicity. At its root are qualities that contrast markedly with our present culture: co-operation instead of competition, generosity instead of greed, patience instead of haste and sufficiency instead of indulgence. And, of course, underlying it all there is the mysterious and awesome teaching of Love as not just virtue or emotion but as of the very essence, *being with* not apart from, a teaching of the very connectedness of life.

In a sense, then, we do have a choice. Not whether to move towards simplicity – for, in reality, that is no longer a matter of choice – but whether to challenge and change convention, to have the courage to let go of the myth of a profligate prosperity and, in breaking loose from the hidden compulsion of consumerism, to rediscover a foundation for well-being. To do this we have to awaken our senses so that we can see the emperor's nakedness and hear once more the timeless teachings of how to live well.

Such a change in our way of being will not come easily. For most of us, not only will it require a painful breaking of habit but also a willingness to accept a discipline and a slower pace, which are both unfashionable. We live in a society that associates freedom with individual rights. Most especially there are the much-trumpeted "rights of the consumer". Of course, such rights are more apparent than real. For as Edward Bernays would no doubt have recognised, consumerism requires the illusion of the "right to consume" but in reality seeks to enslave rather than liberate. It certainly has nothing to say about the freedom that might come from consuming less; the delight that might come from being able to let go of the incessant chatter of our senses to find, in Eliot's words, the still point where the dance is – freedom *from* self rather than freedom *for* self.

Indeed, such a proposition is so subversive and counter to the dogma of our time that it may be difficult for us to accept that attentiveness and slowness might add to our well-being, that silence and compassion might bring happiness. But this of course, *is* the teaching of the sacred tradition of holiness – to become whole, to be fully ourselves and at one with all that *is*, we have to learn to let go and *dwell* in the Divine with an open heart.

Such a dwelling requires a certain spontaneity, a vivacity of spirit, but above all else it requires an uncommon capacity for slowness. Like many of us I suspect, for most of my life I have had an obsession with "doing" and it is only recently that I have come to see this as a mighty hindrance. Some while ago I read the following extract from *The Curly Pyjama Letters*[7] on the notice board at Schumacher College in Devon[8]:

> Dear Vasco, in response to your question "What is worth doing and what is worth having?" I would like

---

[7] Michael Leunig, *The Curly Pyjama Letters*, (2001).
[8] www.schumachercollege.org.uk

to say this. *It is worth doing nothing and having a rest;* in spite of all the difficulty it may cause, you must rest Vasco – otherwise you will become RESTLESS! I believe the world is sick with exhaustion and dying of restlessness.... Yours sleepily, Mr Curly

At once, I can hear the outraged voices of those who can see there is much to be done and who, like me, carry the childhood burden of always needing to have something to do. But on reflection, is not Mr. Curly right to point out that our restlessness and consequent fatigue are "ultimately soul destroying as well as earth destroying"?

Again, the great spiritual traditions have understood this and have always taught of the need for attentive silence, for the regular practise of meditation and contemplation. In these traditions such practice is regarded as the very foundation of true action. And for people who have had the privilege of living, even for a short while, with those who most patently lead a holy life, it will be clear that the distinction between contemplation and action is a false one. Indeed, it seems to me it is our thoughtless and compulsive urge to "do" that so often leads to harm.

What is required is a confident statement of the possibility of greater simplicity and its delight, working it out in our daily lives, with a vigilant resistance to the dominant propaganda of growing consumerism. In my experience this can be very uncomfortable because so much of our present culture is taking us in the opposite direction; but this discomfort is as nothing to the evident catastrophic consequences of our failure to change our lives and find a more sustainable path. To find simplicity, what we need is reflection, attentiveness, compassion and courage.

We live in a world in which there is a grotesque conjunction of poverty and plenty. On the one hand, we are rich and rush to acquire the next promise of happiness – the mobile that plays music and shows us pictures, the second and third holiday in places that were until recently too distant to dream of, the face lift, the lip plump and the brow botoxed, the fashion label and, of course, as much as we can possibly drink or eat. On the other hand, and leaving aside the evident poverty and distress of places far away, we are poor – the trains are late and dirty, we cannot afford to pay those who care and teach, people die on trolleys in hospital corridors and more and more children fail to learn to read and write, the roads are congested and littered with waste, we have high levels of debt and we feel dis-eased, we face the dangers of climate change and resource depletion and are having to face up to a banking system possibly holed below the water line by the credit crunch.

In such a world, a world in which there seems to be an ever-growing gap between image and reality, there is an urgent need to see things as they really are. The difficulty is, we have been told that "reality" is the very stuff of our fantasy – that "the real world" is indeed made up of, dependent upon, an ever increasing round of material aspiration and acquisition, that even if the image ever eludes us it is nevertheless real. We have the right to be satisfied and we should sue if we are not. This is a world of "my" and "mine". It is a world in which we are to maximise our personal satisfaction – but never be contented.

At a personal and at a global level, this is a world of deep dissatisfaction. But the Quaker testimony on simplicity is about more than this. It is not just about having too much. It is also intimately linked with the testimony on equality – if I have more, does that mean someone else must have less; and with the testimony on our relationship with Nature – am I asking for more than Nature can provide and sustain? Furthermore, there is the question of whether my life is so complicated and demanding that I neglect my life with God. As *Advices and Queries* 28 says:

> Every stage of our lives offers fresh opportunities. Responding to divine guidance, try to discern the right time to undertake or relinquish responsibilities without undue pride or guilt. Attend to what love requires of you, which may not be great busyness.[9]

Or as we have already heard from the Buddha: "A seeker of peace should drop the world's bait".[10] And it is captured in these words from the Quaker Thomas Kelly:

> This amazing simplification comes when we "center down", when life is lived with singleness of eye, from a holy Center where the breath and stillness of Eternity are heavy upon us and we are wholly yielded to Him. Some of you know this holy, recreating Center of eternal peace and joy and live in it day and night. Some of you may see it over the margin and wistfully long to slip into that amazing Center where the soul is at home with God. Be very faithful to that wistful longing. It is the Eternal Goodness calling you to return Home, to feed upon green pastures and walk beside still waters and live in the peace of the Shepherd's presence. It is the life *beyond* fevered strain. We are called beyond strain, to peace and power and joy and love and thorough abandonment of self. We are called to put our hands trustingly in His hand and walk the holy way, in no anxiety assuredly resting in Him.[11]

---

[9]   *Advices and Queries* 28, QFP,1.02.28.
[10] *The Connected Discourses of the Buddha*, translated by Bhikkhu Bodhi, (2000), 90.
[11] Thomas R. Kelly, *A Testament of Devotion*, (1992; 1st published 1941), 46.

Chapter 4

On Peace[1]

Search out whatever in your own way of life may
contain the seeds of war.[2]

In March 2003, I was to go to America to give a lecture on
the perennial philosophy. But then the war in Iraq came and
I decided not to go. I wish I could have been clearer in my
own mind about it all, but I found myself torn by contending
feelings. On the one hand, I wanted to make the visit and to
give my lecture. On the other hand, I felt that the distraction
of the war made it difficult for people to do more than watch
its terrible unfolding day by day on the screens of their
televisions.

As it happens, ever since the first of the peace marches,
I had felt a strange emptiness, a sense that something was
missing. Of course, I knew that such public action was
important, and I admire those who decide to protest in
this way. But somehow I was then, and I have been since,
overcome by a feeling it will never be enough. For it seems
to me that those of us for whom war is simply not an option

---

[1] Much of this text first appeared as an essay entitled "Peace Talk" in the
Friends Quarterly, vol.35, no.1, (Jan. 2006). Reprinted with the editor's
kind permission.

[2] *Advices and Queries* 31, QFP 1.02.31.

have a special responsibility not only to protest but also to say what we *will* do in the face of tyranny and oppression, wherever it is found.

The war came. And then the war went away – or at least the part we normally call "war". Now we are left with the part we normally call "peace" – except that guns continue to be fired and people continue to die. When does war start and when does it end and when does it begin again? More especially, when are we at war and when are we at peace?

Besieged by all of this and, indeed, by the incessant noise of war, I found myself returning for sustenance to the wellspring of my Quaker tradition and not least again to the first of our *Advices & Queries*:

> Take heed, dear Friends, to the promptings of love and truth in your hearts...[3]

At the centre of this advice there is, of course, not only a strong commitment *against* war but also a strong commitment *to* nonviolence and peace.[4] But when I looked, I found we are asked to go further than this: we are urged not only to stand in opposition to war but to live "in the virtue of that life and power that takes away the occasion of all wars".[5] This requires not simply that we should be against war "out there" but that we do not harbour within our hearts the seeds of war. Furthermore, it requires us to hold true to that most difficult of Christ's teachings, that we love our enemies. Our *Advices and Queries* ask us:

---

[3] *A&Q* 1, *QFP* 1.02.1.
[4] See *QFP*, Chapter 24.
[5] *QFP*, 24.01, a quotation from George Fox, 1651.

... Do you faithfully maintain our testimony that war and the preparation for war are inconsistent with the spirit of Christ? Search out whatever in your own way of life may contain the seeds of war. Stand firm in our testimony, even when others commit or prepare to commit acts of violence, yet always remember that they too are the children of God.[6]

And it is worth noting that this advice is followed immediately by one that underlines our personal responsibility:

Bring into God's light those emotions, attitudes and prejudices in yourself which lie at the root of destructive conflict, acknowledging your need for forgiveness and grace. ...[7]

This is difficult enough but, as I have said, it seems to me the real challenge for us is this: since we protest against war we have an awesome responsibility to be clear about what it is that we propose as an alternative.

However, we immediately run into an impasse. For those who challenge convention do not set the ground for debate. The ground is set by those who accept convention and will only argue within its bounds. "Another solution" simply cannot, therefore, be found unless that ground is abandoned, those bounds broken.

For example, presented with tyranny and suffering, the conventional language of war focuses upon the former, most often identifying the enemy in a highly personalised way. But perhaps there is another way of looking at such a problem. We could say that in Iraq the focus on Saddam Hussein was the wrong focus. We could say that although they are connected,

---

[6]   *Advices and Queries* 31, QFP, 1.02.31.
[7]   *A&Q* 32, QFP, 1.02.32.

the real problem in Iraq was not the tyranny of Saddam Hussein, but suffering, the poverty, illness and homelessness of the Iraqi people. At great cost, convention brought arms and men to bear down upon the tyrant, with aid as an aftermath. But why is it not possible for nations to come together, much more than they do at present, to make much greater effort directly to tackle the suffering "a priori"? Irrespective of the controlling regime, can we imagine a United Nations workforce having the collective authority to move into countries that suffer in this way and provide food, shelter and medicines, wherever possible providing the local people with the means to help themselves – and maintaining that support for as long as is needed? And if not, are we not letting the limits of convention stifle us?

Of course, much good work is already underway, but what I am calling for is such a shift in awareness that the present efforts would be increased not less than tenfold. And who would pay? We would pay. For the truth is that our present lifestyles are already enjoyed at the cost of those that suffer. It is not our wealth alone; it is theirs also. We should share it with them. Would we feast with a starving child at the door? Well, at present we do so all of the time, the only difference being that, for those of us in the West, the child is usually many miles away. The truth is, there really is no solution that does not carry a cost. After all, we paid for the war in Iraq and no doubt we shall be expected to pay for the continuing "war against terrorism".

In all of this, I hear that haunting teaching of Christ:

> For I was an hungred, and ye gave me no meat: I was thirsty, and ye gave me no drink:
> I was a stranger, and ye took me not in: naked and ye clothed me not: sick and in prison, and ye visited me not.
> Then shall they also answer him, saying, Lord, when saw we thee an hungred, or athirst, or a stranger, or

naked, or sick, or in prison, and did not minister unto thee?

Then shall he answer them, saying, Verily I say unto you, Inasmuch as ye did it not to one of the least of these, ye did it not to me.[8]

So, there can be no excuses. We are charged with removing "the occasion of all wars"[9] and I think the following extract from *Quaker Faith & Practice*, written in 1915, proclaims the matter clearly:

Meeting at a time when the nations of Europe are engaged in a war of unparalleled magnitude, we have been led to recall the basis of the peace testimony of our religious Society. It is not enough to be satisfied with a barren negative witness. ... We must search for a positive, vital, constructive message.[10]

The text goes on to propose that the solution is to be found in Christ's message of love and the "indwelling Christ", which calls to "the peaceable spirit and the rule of love in all the broad and manifold relations of life".

Using the words of George Fox quoted above, it ends as follows:

Thus while love, joy, peace, gentleness and holiness are the teaching of the life and death of our Lord, it is to these that we are also impelled by the indwelling of the Divine in men. As this spirit grows within us, we shall realise increasingly what it is to live in the virtue of that life and power which takes away the occasion of all wars.

---

[8] Matthew 25:42–45.
[9] *QFP* 24.01: a quotation from George Fox, 1651.
[10] *QFP*, 24.08.

By emphasising this aspect of the problem, we are in effect recognising that the "root of destructive conflict"[11] lies within us and in the values that inform our day-to-day life. We have to ask ourselves, therefore, whether or not the seeds of violence lie hidden within the ground of our personal relationships, our work, the form of our governance and economy. Unless and until we do so, we are unlikely to be able to find and sustain the way that "takes away the occasion of all wars".

I know there is already a body of work that has explored this territory and I am embarrassed at my own ignorance of the work to which good people devote their lives. But I feel it will never be enough to proclaim institutional solutions unless and until we have accepted the need to look deep within ourselves. At a recent Quaker meeting, an elderly Friend quoted from the Anglican prayer book: "O God, make clean our hearts within us. And take not thy Holy Spirit from us." There is much wisdom in this and I feel we shall never be able to overcome the violence in the big and distant things until we are able to overcome the violence in the small things that are close at hand.

It matters how we see the world. For, as mentioned before, the Buddha taught us:

> What we are today comes from our thoughts of yesterday, and our present thoughts build our life of tomorrow: our life is the creation of our mind.[12]

So if there is violence, conflict and aggression, we should show no surprise since we have come to believe in violence, conflict and aggression. Indeed, we have been persuaded that violence, conflict and aggression are not only inherent in us but define us. As long as this ignorance rules our lives, we shall continue

---

[11] *Advices and Queries* 31, *QFP*, 1.02.31.
[12] *The Dhammapada*, v.1.

to live in conditions of violence, conflict and aggression for, as we have seen, what we take to be true becomes manifest both within us and around us.

If then it all depends upon what we take to be true and what we choose to take an interest in, I have come to realise that I am not interested in war. For war is not true in the sense that peace is true. And so I have taken a vow not to discuss it. I am no longer interested in protesting about something I am *against*, but only in proposing something I am *for*. I am *for* peace and I am for it for a number of good reasons.

Firstly, I am for peace because I believe this is our natural state. I believe that at root we have a tendency to seek to be at peace both within ourselves and with those around us. It seems to me that our families and our work are based upon endless acts of co-operation and collaboration, and over millions of years those who survived have done so by learning to fit into their habitat – physical, social, economic or cultural. However much we may seek to do things well, we also want to belong and to be a part of this co-operation. And it also seems to me that it is precisely when we move away from this, or when this harmony is disrupted, that we are most often endangered and distressed.

Secondly, it seems to me that reality is not made up of separateness but of relatedness, itself a manifestation of a mysterious balance and order. It is forever in flux, but this natural state of oneness is something to which we always seek to return, not to capture but to dwell within.

Thirdly, I am struck by the common and timeless teachings of peace, gentleness, compassion and the caring for others. The great teachings – whether the ten perfections of Buddhism, Rumi's songs of the beloved or Christ's parable of the Good Samaritan – tell us that to be skilful, alive or full of grace is to be full of love – at peace with ourselves and with others, at peace with nature and at peace with that great mystery which some call God.

The real challenge, then, is to make a robust and persuasive case for peace, to do what we can to learn the skills of peacefulness, to practise it and to be aware of the presence of peace and compassion in us and around us. Surely that is enough for one lifetime. For the Buddha taught:

> Better than a thousand useless words is one single
> word that gives peace.[13]

I shall end here with two observations that came from an informal lunchtime seminar with colleagues at the University of Maryland in April 2008.

First we discussed the way in which we talk about peace, and the suggestion was that our focus should be upon peace and not conflict – upon peace for and of itself and not merely as a remedy for conflict. The question that might be asked is this: "What is it that brings people together?" rather than "How do we move from conflict to peace?" Such enquiry would take love as being of our true nature, and take more interest in how wars end than in how they begin. This would study how people live and work together well, and would advocate the teaching of peace and ethics in school – the history of co-operation rather than the history of warfare. It would challenge the use of warlike language in all discourse, challenging, for example, phrases such as "the battle against cancer". As "sexism" and "racism" are now challenged so "warism", too, would come to be challenged.

The second matter was for us to recognise the reality of conflict but we were challenged to probe more deeply to understand it better. We were required to ask the question "What is conflict for?" Since it is part of our humanity, what is its function in our lives; how does it enable us? We need to be attentive to the arising of feelings of conflict – perhaps from

---

[13] *The Dhammapada*, v.100.

fear or a sense of injustice. If we were better able to identify and understand such feelings, we might then be more able to manage the arising of conflict before it erupts into violence.

Knowing that there are good young people asking these questions must, surely, be grounds for hope that we can discover and nurture the "seeds of peace" in our lives.

Chapter 5

Prayer, Darkness and Discourse[1]

Do you try to set aside times of quiet for openness...?[2]

The place of prayer is a precious habitation...[3]

It is said that Christ gives prayer to the one who prays.[4] It took me a long time to discover prayer. It took me a long time to come to its meaning, to know its presence. And even now I am just at the beginning of a journey.

Prayer came to me from Love; Love came to me from learning to see things as they really are; and seeing things as they really are came to me from discovering my profound ignorance. How long have I journeyed, Lord, when I should have known, really known, from that Sufi tale given to me such a long time ago,[5] how Truth lay close at hand? Forgive my stupidity.

---

[1] Parts of this chapter are taken from *The Honeysuckle and the Rose*, a lecture given at the New York School of Interior Design, April 2008.

[2] *Advices & Queries* 3, QFP, 1.02.3.

[3] *QFP* 20.10; from John Woolman, *Journal*, 1770, and quoted in Reginald Reynolds, *The Wisdom of John Woolman*, (1988, 1st published 1948), 112.

[4] Given to me by my friend Father Silouan, thinking of Romans 8:26,27.

[5] Idries Shah, 'The Initiation of Malik Dinar', *Tales of the Dervishes*, (1982), 148–151.

But now I see that whether in the blessed silence of a Quaker Meeting, the guru yoga of the Tibetan monk or the ceaseless prayer of the Orthodox hesychast, the truth of prayer lies not so much in the object of prayer as in the state of being of the one who prays. In prayer we let go of the self and turn the heart to that which is at one and, at the same time, both familiar and Unknowable.

Some little while ago, I was privileged to meet Rabjam Rinpoche, the grandson of the great Tibetan Lama, Dilgo Khyentse Rinpoche. During this meeting, Rabjam Rinpoche gave me a number of books containing teachings of his grandfather. One of these books, *The Wish-Fulfilling Jewel*[6] provides a teaching on the practice of Tibetan guru yoga according to the Longchen Nyinhthig tradition. As I read it I could see that it was, in essence, very similar to the Jesus prayer practised by Orthodox Christian hesychasts.

Now there are important differences, of course, not least the fact that the Tibetan yoga envisages at first an actual present-day guru, while the ceaseless prayer of the hesychast invokes the Son of God. Nevertheless, the similarities are significant. Both teach us to envisage the object of prayer, the guru or Jesus, and to imagine bringing the presence of this figure into the heart. In both, the result of such practice is to be filled with light and to see more clearly. Both use a repeated phrase. In the guru yoga it is the mantra of "Om Äh Hüng Vajra Guru Padma Siddhi Hüng", which means, "Homage to the enlightened powers of the Lotus-born Guru".[7] In the Jesus prayer, the words are "Lord Jesus Christ, Son of God, have mercy upon me".

The essence of each of these prayers is to call upon the guru or the Divine. However, in each case the purpose of doing so is not primarily to praise from afar but rather to open one's heart, and to be filled with the Light of their presence.

---

6   Dilgo Khyenstse, *The Wish-Fulfilling Jewel*, (2004).
7   Taken from a translation given on www.dzogchen.org.

George Fox, of course, spoke often of this Light, and the practice of "ceaseless prayer" is also taken up by Thomas Kelly, extracted in *Quaker Faith and Practice*:[8]

> How then shall we lay hold of that Life and Power, and live the life of prayer without ceasing? By quiet, persistent practice in turning all our being, day and night, in prayer and inward worship and surrender, towards Him who calls in the deeps of our souls.

This text continues about the need to make such prayer a constant part of our daily lives, from rising to retiring, and using pauses in the day to "surrender to Him who is within".

I find this teaching to be most comforting; to know there is within each one of us a still and quiet place of love, a place we can turn to at any moment of the day or night. Most of us, perhaps, are not very experienced or disciplined in our prayer life and are somewhat overcome by teachings which involve the remembrance of particular words and phrases. Finding our place in blessed silence and waiting upon God with an open and humble heart is also not easy but, as a Quaker, it speaks to my condition.

———————

Then there is the matter of silence:

> Drop Thy still dews of quietness,
> Till all our strivings cease;
> Take from our souls the strain and stress,
> And let our ordered lives confess
> The beauty of Thy peace.

———————

[8] *QFP* 2.22.

These words from the nineteenth century American Quaker John Greenleaf Whittier are one of the memories of my childhood, memories that have remained with me as I have grown older. They return to me again and again, in odd and sometimes unexpected moments, but most especially they return during periods of quietness, for they seem to capture something of the essence of that Divine Mystery which some call God.

For many years, I could not bring myself easily to use the word "God". I found that when I did so it acted as a block to my sense of the Divine. As a "birthright" Quaker I was brought up in a family familiar with God but somehow, over time, over the years, the word had taken on a meaning at odds with both my head and my heart. It had come to mean an "old man on a cloud" sitting in judgement upon a sinful humanity, someone who in a rather managerial sense had created the world but remained apart from it.

The problem was so grave that one day, quite late in life, I went to see an elder of my Quaker meeting. Much to my surprise – and I have to say relief – she did not seem to be at all disturbed about the problem. She admitted that she really did not know what was meant by the word "God" but she supposed that "it had to do with Love". This so resonated with my own intuition that the block was at once removed and led me in time to see that Love – not as virtue or as emotion but as being of the nature of reality – was not only of the essence but was to be experienced most deeply in the attentive stillness and silence of meditation.

Silence is, of course, at the root of all the great spiritual traditions. It is the very language of the inner world of contemplation and in the Islamic tradition it is regarded as "the garden of meditation".[9] For me, however, the place of

---

[9] A quotation of 'Ali contained in *Maxims of 'Ali*, Lahore, Ashraf Publication, n.d. 32 and quoted in Whitall N. Perry, *A Treasury of Traditional Wisdom*, Fons Vitae, (2000), 526.

silence has been found most especially in the teachings and practices of Christianity and of Buddhism.

There is a long tradition of silent prayer and contemplation in the Christian tradition. In the Old Testament, God speaks to the prophet Elijah:

> And he said, Go forth, and stand upon the mount before the LORD. And, behold, the LORD passed by, and a great and strong wind rent the mountains, and brake in pieces the rocks before the Lord; *but* the LORD *was* not in the wind; and after the wind an earthquake; *but* the LORD *was* not in the earthquake.
>
> And after the earthquake a fire; *but* the LORD *was* not in the fire: and after the fire a still small voice.
>
> And it was so, when Elijah heard *it*, that he wrapped his face in his mantle, and went out, and stood in the entering of the cave. And, behold, *there came* a voice unto him, and said, What doest thou here Elijah?[10]

We are told that Jesus often withdrew from the noise and bustle of the town and went up into the mountains to give his teaching. Silence was very much a part of the tradition of the early Christian Desert Fathers and of the later mystics such as Hildegard of Bingen, Julian of Norwich and Meister Eckhart.[11] Furthermore, if silence is not so much a central part of modern Western Christianity, where singing, spoken prayer and sermons are more familiar, there remains a contemplative tradition, not least in the monasteries and nunneries of the Anglican and Roman Catholic churches, in profound moments of remembrance, in the lighting of a candle or in moments of private prayer and contemplation.

---

[10] 1 Kings, 19:11–13.

[11] A tradition that is sustained by the World Community for Christian Meditation, St Mark's Myddleton Square, London, EC1R 1XX, 020 7278 2070, uk@wccm.org

Most especially, silence lies at the heart of Quaker worship. Gathered together, without priest or liturgy, Quakers sit quietly and wait upon the Lord. During the meeting there may be ministry, but it is not uncommon for a meeting for worship to pass without anyone speaking. Indeed, while Friends are encouraged to accept the responsibility of ministry, they are urged to be sure that their ministry comes from the heart:

> Do not assume that vocal ministry is never to be your part. Faithfulness and sincerity in speaking, even very briefly, may open the way to fuller ministry from others. When prompted to speak, wait patiently to know that the leading and the time are right, but do not let your sense of your own unworthiness hold you back. Pray that your ministry may arise from deep experience, and trust that words will be given to you. Try to speak audibly and distinctly, and with sensitivity to the needs of others. Beware of speaking predictably or too often, and of making additions towards the end of a meeting when it was well left before.[12]

And, if they speak for too long, they may be reminded quietly by an elder of the meeting that perhaps a period of silence would now be welcomed!

In this silence, we Quakers listen to our innermost thoughts and feelings. As I have mentioned, in our *Advices and Queries* we are given this guidance:

> Take heed, dear Friends, to the promptings of love and truth in your hearts. Trust them as the leadings of God whose Light shows us our darkness and brings us new life.[13]

_____

[12] *Advices & Queries* 13, QFP 1.02.13.
[13] *Advices & Queries* 1, QFP 1.02.1.

Also this:

> In worship we enter into communion with God and
> respond to the promptings of the Holy Spirit. Come
> with heart and mind prepared. Pray silently as you
> gather together that you may all be drawn into the
> spirit of adoration and communion...[14]

The stillness and silence of a Quaker meeting speaks of the
unknowable and inexpressible mystery of the Divine and,
in the presence of this mystery, it speaks of acceptance and
humility.

Somewhat at the other end of the spectrum of the Christian
tradition, in the ornate and splendid tradition of Orthodoxy,
with its icons, incense, chanting and liturgy, there is also
a tradition of silent contemplation. This is known as the
Hesychast Way and is described with great beauty by the
late Philip Sherrard in his book *Christianity: Lineaments of a
Christian Tradition*.[15] Hesychasm is part of the tradition of the
Eastern Christian world and comes from the Greek *hesychia*
meaning stillness, denoting the state that it induces.

As with other forms of meditation, the initial state of
hesychast practice consists in reversing the process of
dispersed thought and self-destructive activity to bring the
mind and heart to a state of stillness:

> Through a rigorous method of vigilance –
> watchfulness – in which the root of each thought is
> scrutinized and assessed, it becomes possible to strip

---

[14] *A&Q 9, QFP* 1.02.9
[15] Philip Sherrard, *Christianity: Lineaments of a Sacred Tradition*, (1998).

the mind bare and to awaken a true understanding by freeing it from the thoughts and images that usually possess it and prevent it from seeing and experiencing its own inner reality. It is only then that we are in a position to recover our natural state, to breathe once again the air of divinity and to enjoy the peace we lost through turning our attention outwards, away from ourselves, on to the world of things and objects.[16]

Descending into the heart by means of the invocation of the divine name in the form known as the Jesus Prayer, we become, says Philip Sherrard, conscious of the treasure, the divine presence, hidden there. Here we find a correspondence between "the physical breath, which gives rhythm to and sustains life, and the divine Breath":

> In this way the in-breath, led downwards into the heart, acts as the vehicle through which the intellect descends into the heart, becomes conscious of the divine life hidden there, and brings us into union with the source of our inmost being and identity; while the out-breath vehicles the divine grace with which it is now infused to all our members and by extension to the world of living things about us. It is thus that the invocation becomes truly the prayer of the heart.[17]

Throughout his writing, Philip Sherrard makes it clear that silent contemplation is not an add-on to other forms of worship but, rather, the foundation upon which all else stands. Suggesting that true knowledge requires us to become one with the Divine, he makes it clear that this must be through the practice of contemplation – the Hesychast Way. This is an

---

[16] Philip Sherrard, *Christianity*, 247–248.
[17] *Christianity*, 249.

affirmation of the proposition that contemplation is a necessary precursor to true understanding and thus to true action.

> ...for contemplation is essentially the action through which we are led to a knowledge of our true identity and being and hence the true identity and being of other things as well... It is not (then) that contemplation is opposed to action: not only is it in itself a form – the highest form – of action, but also unless all other actions are informed by the knowledge that it embraces they will be performed in ignorance... To act well, we must first know. Thus, while contemplation and action are complementary, they are not on an equal footing: contemplation must precede action.[18]

Despite the obvious differences between the bare simplicity of Quakerism and the ornate liturgy and services of Orthodoxy, they share two important characteristics – a direct encounter with the Divine and a love of silence.

Here is my recollection of a visit to the Monastery of Vatopedi on Mount Athos.

It is early morning and the wooden *talanto*, said to have been used by Noah to summon the animals and birds into the ark, is now being struck in the courtyard of the Monastery of Vatopedi on Mount Athos as we, in turn, are summoned to the Divine Liturgy. We enter the katholikon, the church of the Annunciation of the Virgin Mary, pass through the outer chapel or narthex, and take our place in the nave among the other pilgrims and the workmen who live at the monastery while they help to restore its ancient buildings.

Coming into the dark from the bright sunshine of the courtyard, it takes a while to adjust. But when we do, our

---

[18] *Christianity*, 246–247.

eyes are drawn upwards to the great dome of the katholikon and the golden corona that hangs from it, lit by candles and accompanied on either side by large chandeliers, each one also golden and candle lit. Before us is the iconostasis, a high wooden screen with many icons but especially the figures of Mary the Mother of God, Christ and John the Baptist. And in front, standing upon an easel or resting against a pillar are the Madonna and Child and an icon of the Hospitality of Abraham, in which Abraham and Sarah are accompanied by the three angels that to the Orthodox represent the Trinity.

From the apse on each side of the transept comes the chant of the monks. On either side, bearded and robed in black, they stand in a group around an upright reading-desk upon which the books of the liturgy are laid. Their chant is sonorous, the underlying drone of the *ison* forming a foundation for the melody, the undulating chant of worship and prayer, which passes from one side to the other. Some monks stand or half sit in the stalls that surround each apse, while others appear to walk in and out in no particular order. Behind the iconostasis, in the sanctuary, the priests perform their holy tasks, coming out through curtained doors from time to time to read from the scriptures or spread the aroma of incense upon us all.

Eventually, monks and lay people alike form a procession to venerate the icons, crossing themselves from left to right and from the forehead to the ground. Many monks also perform modest prostrations, the younger with more vigour than the older, facing east, west, south and north. And then, for the communion or *koinonia*, the priest, using a long spoon, takes from the chalice small pieces of bread dipped in wine and places them into the upturned mouths of the faithful. The service that has built to a climax now recedes, and lay people and monks walk out into the sunlit courtyard.

For a Quaker brought up in the plainness and simplicity of our meeting for worship, you might suppose that this would all be something of a shock, even intense discomfort. Indeed,

I was quite prepared to feel oppressed. But actually I felt strangely at home.

In my local meeting, we might allow ourselves a vase of flowers, taken from the garden of one Friend or another, but otherwise we limit ourselves to a rectangle of chairs and benches and a table upon which are placed a few books, the Bible, our *Advices and Queries* and a copy of *Quaker Faith and Practice*. We sit in silence, with no priests and certainly no chanting. From time to time, any member of the meeting may stand to offer a prayer or share a thought but, often, there will be nothing more than a deep and shared silence. This is our way.

But behind a superficial difference, there is truly much in common. For in the Orthodox service, I have found myself to be very much at one with God. The liturgy is being performed before me but, as in a Quaker meeting for worship, its effect is to draw me into a state of stillness and prayer that prepares me to wait upon the Lord with an open and humble heart. The chanting and incense, the icons and candles may be mesmeric but, for the Orthodox monks and lay people, the ritual, the chant and the icons have no meaning except as a direct expression of the Divine. When the icons are venerated, it is the Divine presence that is worshipped and not the icons themselves.

Furthermore, the silence of Quakerism is matched by the silent prayer of the Orthodox hesychasts, inwardly repeating over and over again the Jesus Prayer: "Lord Jesus Christ, Son of God, have mercy upon me". These solitary and often elderly monks can sometimes be seen sitting quietly in a corner during the Divine Liturgy, perhaps waiting to be inwardly "refreshed" by the bread and wine of the *koinonia*. Indeed, some will say that the drone of the chant represents the ever-recurring sound of the Jesus Prayer and that a life of inner prayer requires that there is also, albeit elsewhere, the outer performance of the Divine Liturgy.

In any event, both Quakers and Orthodox seek to awaken that of God in our hearts so we can better act aright in our daily lives, finding God's will and expressing love and compassion in all things. In taking communion, the Orthodox receive that which is an expression of the Divine so they may turn their hearts to the Lord. For Quakers, the Divine is ever-present but is awakened in the silence of worship. For both, there must be both prayer and a willingness to turn to God.

We do not meet as strangers but as brothers and sisters. As Quakers, we propose that there is "that of God in everyone". Which surely is also what the Orthodox liturgy is celebrating. Quakers in silent waiting, Orthodox in the veneration of the icons and in the taking of the bread and wine. Inwardly or outwardly, each one of us seeks to find that of God within ourselves.

Of all the great spiritual traditions, Buddhism is where we most notably find the teaching of silent attentiveness. Such meditation forms a central part of the life of the monks and nuns of the different Buddhist traditions and, in the West, it is part of the daily practice of those who "take refuge" in the Buddha. Indeed, in certain schools of Zen Buddhism such practices are simply described as *zazen* or "just sitting".

One of the most important teachings on meditation given by the Buddha is the *Ānāpānasati Sutta* or *The Mindfulness of Breathing*.[19] Here, such meditation is described as being "of great fruit and benefit". Sitting in stillness and bringing one's attention to the inflow and outflow of the breath, you come to a point of tranquil alertness. The constant chattering of the mind becomes quiet and, in time and with practice, you find

---

[19] *The Middle Length Discourse of the Buddha*, translated by Bhikkhu Ñānamoli and Bhikkhu Bodhi, (1995), 941.

yourself in a realm of detachment and clarity, a condition in which you are at one with all that is – the suchness of life.

This condition of mindfulness is not, however, something for the meditation mat alone, but may be practised whether standing or walking or lying down. Indeed, it may be practised at any moment of the day or night in whatever you are doing. There is the story of the monk who went to see his Master and said to him, "Master, how shall I find enlightenment?" The Master replied, "Have your breakfast." The monk said, "But I have had my breakfast." "Then wash your bowl," said the Master. At this point, the monk was enlightened. Today, this story might relate to how we drive a car or answer a telephone but the teaching is that mindfulness is to be part of our lives at all times.

Indeed, mindfulness is so much a part of the Buddhist way that it takes its place as part as the Fourth Noble Truth, the Noble Eightfold Path: right understanding, right thought, right speech, right action, right livelihood, right effort, right mindfulness and right concentration. This path is what enables us to let go of craving and attachment, and thus leads to the cessation of suffering; its foundation is tranquil alertness.

In each one of the great religious traditions, then, silence is much more than a form of worship. It is a way of life, or rather it is a way of being. It challenges the contemporary focus on "doing" and speaks of the need for reflection as the basis of action. It is the foundation of attentiveness and the listening heart that leads to compassion. It requires us to find and nurture the pauses in life, the spaces between those moments of action that seem so much to determine every day.

———————————

In all these religious traditions, there is much talk of Light – enlightenment, illumination, the radiance of the Divine – and in our Quaker tradition, George Fox urged us to "stand in the Light". But what then of darkness, since we all know and experience darkness – both physically in the passage of night and day and the seasons, Spring and Summer giving way to Autumn and Winter, and metaphorically in the darkness of the soul.

Our ancient forebears knew this well and, in the Celtic tradition, believed that light arose out of darkness. Their days started with eventide – just as we celebrate Christmas Eve or New Year's Eve on the evening before Christmas or New Year's Day – and their year started not on 1st January but with the festival of Samhain, the evening of 31st October that we now celebrate as Halloween or All Souls, the beginning of Winter. And it has always seemed to me a miracle – and certainly a mystery – that the seed planted into the ground in the Autumn should be transformed in the darkness of Winter into the shoot that sprouts in the returning light of Spring.

I had been pondering on this for some time when, as if by chance, a Friend stood up in my local meeting for worship and read the following passage from *Quaker Faith and Practice*, by the early Quaker James Nayler:

> Art thou in Darkness? Mind it not, for if thou dost it will fill thee more, but stand still and act not, and wait in patience till Light arises out of Darkness to lead thee.[20]

I was struck by the phrase "and wait in patience till Light arises out of Darkness to lead thee", for it seemed to me then and seems to me now that this can help us to understand the deeply embedded relationship between Light and Darkness – that Light arises out of Darkness in just the way our forebears understood; that Darkness is not to be shunned or feared but

---

[20] *QFP*, 21.65.

seen as the ground of Light; that Divine Love is present in both the Darkness and the Light; and that this is true for us both personally and as a universal working principle.

———————

Then there is the matter of "discourse". For the Buddha, this was a matter of great importance and "Right Speech" is one of the main steps in the Noble Eightfold Path. In a society where written text was unknown and all communication was oral, this seems bound to be so. Indeed, for very many years after his death, the teachings of the Buddha were transmitted by periodic and large gatherings of the *sangha* at which the entire canon was recited and checked for error. The first written version of the teachings did not appear until much later. The teachings of Christ were originally "heard" and not "read" and were apparently not written down for some years after his death. By contrast, we have come to rely not only on written texts, but on texts being instantly recorded, and now electronically processed, stored and disseminated at the touch of a button.

Nevertheless, the way we speak to each other is still important since it shapes the nature of our relationships, whether with lovers, family, friends or colleagues at work or even with strangers. The Buddha's teaching of "Right Speech" is that we should avoid the telling of lies, backbiting and slander, rude and abusive language and idle gossip.[21] The last of these may be the most difficult but can be the most harmful.

As Quakers, we also consider the spoken word. We love silence, are advised to "set aside times of quiet"[22] and in our business meetings, we try to ensure that everyone may speak if they wish to and that no conclusion will be minuted unless and until the text can faithfully express the "feeling of the

———————

[21] Walpola Rahula, *What the Buddha Taught*, (1974), 47.
[22] *Advices & Queries* 3, *QFP*, 1.02.3.

meeting". More specifically, of course, we are urged through our *Advices and Queries* to be mindful about the way in which we speak at our meetings for worship. And perhaps the following gives some sense of the way in which we might not only speak but, more importantly, listen and support others as they try to give voice:

> A Friends' meeting for worship finds no room for debate or for answering (still less for contradicting) one another; if this is desirable, it will be left to another occasion. And if anything should seem to be spoken amiss, the spiritually minded worshipper will have the wit to get to the heart of the message, overlooking crudity and lack of skill in presentation, and so far from giving way to irritation at what seems unprofitable, he will be deeply concerned for his own share in creating the right spiritual atmosphere in which the harm fades out and the good grows. Many a meeting has known this power, transforming what might have been hurtful into a means of grace.[23]

So it would seem that the matter of silence cannot be separated from the matter of discourse. Silence, whether great or small, whether the silence of a meeting for worship or the pause that gives a space for our own or others' thoughts, adds to the quality of all that we have to say and the way in which we say it. That simple rule of "count to ten" before responding to a hurtful remark may be supported by Lao Tzu's saying: "He who knows, does not speak. He who speaks, does not know." In any event, I know I cherish those relationships that work without words; that are able to share silence and quietude.

---

[23] *QFP*, 2.69, a quotation from A Neave Brayshaw, 1921.

Chapter 6

On Sustainability

> We have not yet found the right word or phrase to
> describe this testimony... but it is in the overlap
> of care, respect, love, symbiosis, honouring,
> valuing, hospitality, stewardship, nurture, humility,
> adaptation and accommodation, peaceable living,
> interconnectedness, awe, wonder, relationship,
> harmony, consecration, sacramental or holy living.[1]

Quakers have recently begun to consider their testimony on
what we now call "sustainability". We are still exploring the
right terms, but it seems clear to me that its essence or root lies
in the intricate relationships or, as I prefer, "relatingness", of
the social, the economic and the environmental aspects of our
lives. I use this rather awkward word "relatingness" because
it combines and draws attention to the vital qualities of both
connectivity and reciprocity. It implies a continuous and
purposeful flow of giving and receiving, a realm of mutuality
between each one of us and between all of us and the rest of
the natural world.

The first Quaker testimony on the matter may be in the
following words of John Woolman:

---

[1] Testimonies Committee minute of 2006, in *Testimonies Toolkit*, 55.

So great is the hurry in the spirit of this world, that in aiming to do business quickly, and to gain wealth, the creation at this does loudly groan.[2]

What would he say now!

He also spoke of the need for "tenderness toward all creatures".[3] For in a manner that was radical for his time, he not only drew attention to the cruelty with which animals were often treated, but also to the links between this cruelty, the trade upon which it was based, and the food that was thereby enjoyed in Quaker and non-Quaker homes alike. He saw and spoke of a world of connections, where one apparently separate thing (cruelty to an animal) is linked, directly or indirectly, to another (food on the table). If this is something we all know about now, it was certainly not given much credence in the eighteenth century.

In speaking about "holiness", I have already referred in Chapter 1 to this understanding of linkages or connections as being utterly relevant to our present concerns about "sustainability".[4] And I have suggested that this takes us into territory at the heart of Quaker testimony, for it requires that we consider not simply our outward behaviour – our recycling and the careful use of resources such as water and energy – but also the relationship of the inner and the outer life, that which we hold to be true, and how we thereby live our lives. What is it that causes us to live in one way and not another? What is our "truth" founded upon, and what are the rules of cause and effect that link such truth to everyday action? What is it that lies behind our testimony of sustainability?

---

[2] In Reginald Reynolds, *The Wisdom of John Woolman*, (1988; 1st published 1948), 45.

[3] *Wisdom of John Woolman*, 161–162.

[4] See also David Cadman, *The Roots of Sustainability*, The Prince's Foundation for the Built Environment, 2009

Here is an example of what I mean. As I write,[5] much of what we thought was founded on rock is being shown to be founded on sand. All around, the banks, those temples to thrift and sobriety, are being revealed as no more than casinos. And as the inevitable outcomes of such stupidity and greed unravel before us, severe economic discomfort seems to be on its way. What used to be called "the real world" is looking much more like a fantasy. Some people represent this turmoil as an example of "market failure", as if it is not the basic model that is wrong but only the ways in which it was being managed; so that the road to recovery will be found by a modest readjustment of the status quo. But this will not do. What is happening is not an example of failure but of consequence. The problems we now face are not an accident but are a direct result of particular types of market behaviour.

As John Woolman would have told us, it is important to see that this behaviour is based upon a particular and deliberately chosen set of values – deriving from financial mechanisms and modes of operation that have separated the economic from its social and environmental context. These values, these forms of arrogance, arise from a way of being that has come to dominate what is commonly held to be true. And as a consequence we increasingly seek to find solutions exclusively in the outer, material world of consumerism, greed and exaggerated individuality. But again as Woolman would have noted, the answer to this dilemma cannot be found in the principles and values that have brought us to where we are. If we rely upon them, they will only take us back to the same place. Guidance has to be found elsewhere.

I am at present reading a book about the life and work of Rufus Jones. Born in America in the middle of the nineteenth century, he was one of the most influential Quakers of the twentieth century and, most especially, someone who could

---

[5]   May 2009.

speak of that which I have called a "practical mysticism".[6] What, I wonder, would he have to say about our economic, social and environmental disarray? What would he have to say about this notion of "sustainability"?

Some sense of this response is given in his book *The Inner Life*, which not only speaks of the relationship between the inner and the outer life but also gives a clear understanding of that order of being in which testimony is revealed. In the first sentence of his introduction he says, "There is no inner life that is not also an outer life".[7] Later he emphasises that the holy life is not something that is attained but is something that is searched for and lived. The holy life is about "a thirst for goodness"[8] where "the reach must always exceed the grasp".[9] He describes the holy way as follows:

> Meekness and Mercy and peace-making are high among the qualities that characterize the inner spirit of the kingdom. Patience, endurance, steadfastness, confidence in the eternal nature of things, determination to win by the slow method that is right rather than by the quick and strenuous method that is wrong are other ways of naming meekness. Mercy is tenderness of heart, ability to put oneself in another's place, confidence in the power of love and gentleness, the practice of forgiveness and the joyous bestowal of sympathy. Peace-making is the divine business of drawing men together into unity of spirit and purpose, teaching them to live the love-way, and forming in the very warp and woof of human society the spirit of altruism and loyalty to the higher interests of the group.[10]

---

6   See Introduction.
7   Rufus Jones, *The Inner Life* (1917), v.
8   *Inner Life*, 16.
9   *Inner Life*, 18–19.
10 *Inner Life*, 21–22.

As our own Testimonies Committee has suggested, this is surely the very stuff, the values or principles, upon which we need to build our sustainability testimony.[11]

But perhaps the most relevant aspect of *The Inner Life* is towards the end of the book in the chapter "A Fundamental Spiritual Outlook",[12] where Rufus Jones sets out his expression of the innate holiness of us and the rest of the natural world and the need for us, as a matter of urgency, to "restore faith in the actual reality of God and in the fundamental spiritual nature of the world".[13]

He then gives us an insight not only into the connectedness of a holy sustainability but into what we might call its "intent", when he encourages us to see how all that is – all of the natural world – is suffused with an "intelligent and loving purpose". We should see the world as a "way of love"[14] in which, first and foremost, we must nurture sustainable relationships by participation and by being "persons of the blessed life".[15] Such a way of being, he says, is "the saving salt of the earth" and it will be lost "if the *soul* of religion wanes or dies away and only the outer form of it remains".[16]

Perhaps then our present difficulties of global warming and economic disruption are in part caused by a waning of the soul of religion, by the degradation of the holy life amongst us.

Now there will be many who deride such a notion as a kind of fantasy; who tell us that the real world is something separate from religion; and that all thoughts of holiness are no more than a delusion, a mere sop to our anxiety and discomfort. But there are others who, like Rufus Jones, recognise that nothing could be more real. One such is the

---

[11] See the opening quotation of this chapter.

[12] *Inner Life*, Chapter V.

[13] *Inner Life*, 138.

[14] *Inner Life*, 143.

[15] *Inner Life*, 27.

[16] *Inner Life*, 28. Emphasis in original.

scholar Joseph Milne, a Fellow of the Temenos Academy, who has shared with me some of his work on what is called Natural Law.[17]

Like Rufus Jones' notion of an intelligent and loving purpose, for Joseph Milne the natural world works by way of an impulse (a relationship) both from and towards that which is Good and Whole, "reconciling the realm of Nature with the realm of Grace".[18] In this work, he provides us with a new and quite different insight into how we might consider our relationship with Nature – a different set of principles which might govern such a relationship – through starting from the premise that the created world directly manifests the divine wisdom of God. He then goes on to explain how, at the time of Thomas Aquinas, creation came to be understood as being "not only good but also rational and intelligible"; that:

> Observation of Nature through the natural sciences showed clearly all things had natural tendencies towards full flourishing, and this indicated that all created things, in their growth and activities, sought good as their natural end... [that] Nature was ordered in an ordered and integral way, and tended towards higher orders of synthesis or unity. That is to say, there was the clear evidence of Natural Law in the tendencies of all Nature. ... Nature was intelligent and oriented towards the maximum fullness of being and reason at all levels.[19]

It seems to me that seeing the natural world as the revelation of "the divine Wisdom of God", as lawful, and as the inevitable

---

[17] Joseph Milne, lecture "Society and Natural Law in Thomas Aquinas" at Workshops in Political Theory, Manchester Metropolitan University, 10–12 September 2008 (unpublished).
[18] "Society and Natural Law", 3.
[19] "Society and Natural Law", 2.

expression of a divine cause, goes to the root of our perception of sustainability – of our relationship with Nature – and places upon us a very particular responsibility as we wrestle to come to terms with the damage that we have caused by our own thoughtlessness and profligacy.

But according to this "natural law", two further principles will shape this perception. The first of these is that reality is not fixed but ever under way; and the second is that we must understand how we are a part of a greater whole, that life is wholesome or, as I would say, holy:

> Natural Law, considered in its most essential ground, is itself an embodiment of the natural and just ends of Nature *taken as a single whole*... [and it] is not conceived as a restraint upon things, but rather as the manner in which the being of things may come to its fullest expression and development, both in itself and *for the sake of all things.*[20]

Underlying all of this, then, and underlying our search for an understanding of sustainability, is the fact that the order of this Nature, of which we are but part, is not only divine but rational and purposeful, and it expresses an innate inclination of all things "towards a higher order and unity".[21] This requires not only that we situate ourselves within this natural order as part of an essential inclination towards the fullness of being, but also that our potential destiny depends upon a truthful correspondence with Nature as such, and thus with Natural Law.[22] This must surely be the foundation for our testimony on sustainability.

---

[20] "Society and Natural Law", 3. Emphasis in original.
[21] "Society and Natural Law", 6.
[22] "Society and Natural Law", 7.

At the beginning of this work, I suggested that the root of this testimony on sustainability must be Divine Love; and if we are looking for a defining and guiding principle for our testimony, it too must be Divine Love. However difficult it is to understand the workings of this principle, we must always return to it. It is essentially mysterious – part of that Great Mystery that we sometimes call "God" – and ultimately beyond our complete understanding. Following the path of what I have called "practical mysticism", we should start by attending in love to those things we can understand and know. This means attending to those relationships that are close at hand, whether with each other or with the rest of the natural world, how we grow our food and where we purchase it, what we eat, how we use those resources most dear to us and to our neighbours; it means attending to the pace and expectations of our lives and to our aspirations, so that our testimony does "spring from a place of love".[23]

---

[23] *Testimonies Toolkit*, 4.

Epilogue

At one, in awe and unafraid

If I were to start with the words "Once upon a time", you would recognise straight away that we were entering the realm of story. Story lies at the heart of our being. It is old and familiar, and it is not simply a part of our childhood: most especially, it has formed our mythology, being a way of passing on wisdom and knowledge from one generation to another.

Each one of us, of course, has a story to tell but how shall our story begin? In his book *The Hero with a Thousand Faces*[1] Joseph Campbell says:

> The first stage of the mythological journey [the "call to adventure"] signifies that destiny has summoned the hero and transferred his spiritual center of gravity from within the pale of his society to a zone unknown. This fateful region of both treasure and danger may be variously represented: as a distant land, a forest, a kingdom underground, beneath the waves, or above the sky, a secret island, lofty mountain top, or profound dream state... The adventure may begin as a mere blunder... or still again, one may be only casually strolling, when some passing phenomenon catches the

---

[1] Joseph Campbell, *The Hero with a Thousand Faces*, (1988).

wandering eye and lures one away from the frequented paths of men.

In a world so taken up with rationality and intent, with business plans and five-year strategies, is it not especially thrilling to be told that "the adventure" is always there and always about to begin; that we might stumble upon it when we least expect to?

In some stories, this sudden shift in perception is shown with a strange encounter, perhaps with an animal or a bird or with a shadowy, mysterious or even terrifying figure. In Celtic mythology, for example, one often finds that an adventure is not only started but also governed by the goddess in her triple form of hag, maiden and queen.[2] Thus, in the Mabinogion the goddess Rhiannon draws Pwyll Prince of Dyfed into a world of mystery and the young Gereint is guided by the maiden Enid.[3]

Another version of the beginning of an adventure is that the hero is called forth by a sign: some event dislodges the hero from the comfort of his or her life and changes it forever.[4] The example that Campbell gives is taken from the life of the Buddha who has been been protected from the world by his father, but who sets forth on his path having seen for the first time the suffering of old age, sickness and death and the grace of a holy man.

In any event, it would seem that the inspiration to begin the journey comes most often from a nagging sense of unease or dissatisfaction. As long as we are content and comfortable, why would we set out on an adventure that, according to most myths, is likely to be difficult and dangerous, where much could be gained but all could be lost? And so it is, by whatever

---

[2] I have followed this pattern in my own story of *The King Who Lost His Memory* to be found at www.davidcadman.net

[3] *The Mabinogion*, tr Gwyn and Thomas Jones, (1992).

[4] Joseph Campbell, *The Hero with a Thousand Faces*, (1988), 56.

cause, by chance or by intent, that many of us find ourselves upon a journey, unsure of the destination but compelled to set forth.

The journey, then, is commonly part of story, setting out on a quest – like the Knights of the Round Table entering the dark forest in search of the Grail, or like Odysseus returning home after the Trojan War. The journey, the path, or the way, has come to enter our imagination as part of any adventure. And as such, in all the great traditions, it has been folded into spiritual teaching: we have the Middle Way and the Eightfold Path of Buddhism, the Way of the Tao and, of course, the words of Christ: "I am the way";[5] and in the psalms, "Shew me thy ways, O Lord, teach me thy paths."[6]

There are said to be many paths, some clearly directed and well trodden and others that are lonelier and less well defined. In part by chance and in part by choice, the paths I have taken have tended to be the kind of path you stumble across and have to find for yourself. Brought up as a Quaker, at the very edge of nonconformism and without the company of priests, I learnt to find my own way and to understand as much from silence as from words. This is not to say there was no guidance. On the contrary, as a child and spending many years at a Quaker school, I learnt more than I can say from my father, from teachers and from other Friends. Nevertheless, most often I have found myself on a solitary path.

For much of my life, taken up with work and family, I was not especially aware of this. But now, in later years, in part inspired by the teachings of the Buddha, but remembering the psalms and the passages from the Bible that my father read, I have been drawn back and once again have found myself for the most part walking alone, and content to be so. Perhaps not surprisingly, I have never felt comfortable

---

5   John 14:6.
6   Psalm 24:4.

with religious institutions. Whenever I have come across them, in whatever faith, I have found more discord than harmony, more concern with power and position than with compassion. And yet, somewhat ironically for someone with such a nonconformist upbringing, as far as institutions go I have felt most comfortable in the monasteries of the Orthodox Church. On the Holy Mountain of Mount Athos, amongst the deep chanting of the monks and the glitter of gold and silver, in clouds of incense and before the icons of Christ and Mary, in a most extraordinary way I have experienced the direct presence of the Divine.

Movement is of the essence of a path, and not simply one's own movement either. The path only exists because others have walked it and our walking will keep the path open for others to come. An abandoned path soon becomes no path at all.[7] The Holy Mountain of Mount Athos used to be criss-crossed by well-kept paths, travelled by the monks and by pilgrims, each with their own shrines and resting places. But even here, as more cars have arrived on the Mountain and as pilgrims have been less inclined to walk when they could ride, many of the paths have been lost.[8]

The path remains an important part of all the great teachings. In myth the journey always has a destination; the hero is to discover what Joseph Campbell calls "The Ultimate Boon"[9] – the Grail, the Golden Fleece, the Spring of Youth or even Enlightenment.

In my own case, at some time I have now forgotten but in a moment of unintended clarity, I became aware that the destination of my journey was "to be at one, in awe and

---

[7] Much of this has come from my reading of two books by Stephen Batchelor: *Buddhism Without Beliefs*, (1997), and *Verses From the Center*, (2000), both published by Riverhead.

[8] At the original instigation of the Prince of Wales, the Friends of Mount Athos have for some years been working to clear these footpaths.

[9] Joseph Campbell, *The Hero with a Thousand Faces*, (1988), 172 et seq.

unafraid". And ever since then, this has been my quest. It requires courage and, of course, discipline. But most of all it requires mindfulness, wisdom and compassion. For me, this is the holy life.

I believe that to be "at one" is to be at one with the Divine, the inexpressible and the mysterious. In this state I cannot help but be "in awe"; and I find that in such a place of love there is no fear. This is to be entire and holy.

This holy place, this place of love is found by discipline and the letting go of self, by prayer, meditation and contemplation; it is simple and peaceful and it is a precondition to living in harmony with others and with Nature. We do not have to desert life to find it: it is there in the most unexpected places and if we are attentive, we will find it close at hand amongst the everyday, in the momentary pause, in the "still small voice of calm". It was always there and will be with us even at the end.

Bibliography

Quaker

Dale, Jonathan and others, *Faith in Action: Quaker social testimony*, Quaker Books, 2007 (first published 2000).

Jones, Rufus, *The Inner Life*, The Macmillan Company, New York, 1917.

Kelly, Thomas R., *A Testament of Devotion*, Harper Collins, 1992 (first published 1941).

Penn, William, *Some Fruits of Solitude*, Friends United Press, Richmond, Indiana, 1985.

Quaker Faith & Practice: the book of Christian discipline of the Religious Society of Friends (Quakers) in Britain, 3rd edition, 2005 (first published 1995).

Quaker Peace & Social Witness Testimonies Committee, *Engaging with the Quaker Testimonies: a Toolkit*, Quaker Books, 2007.

Reynolds, Reginald, *The Wisdom of John Woolman*, Quaker Home Service, 1988 (first published 1948).

Buddhist

The Dhammapada, translated by Acharya Buddharakkhita, Buddhist Publication Society, Kandy, Sri Lanka, 1996.

The Dhammapada, translated by Juan Mascaró, Penguin Books, 1973.

The Connected Discourses of the Buddha, translated by Bhikkhu Bodhi, Wisdom Publications, Boston, 2000.

The Middle Length Discourse of the Buddha, translated by Bhikkhu Ñānamoli and Bhikkhu Bodhi, Wisdom Publications, Boston, 1995.

The Long Discourses of the Buddha, translated by Maurice Walshe, Wisdom Publications, Boston, 1995.

Batchelor, Stephen, *Buddhism Without Beliefs*, Riverhead Books, New York, 1997.

Batchelor, Stephen, *Verses from the Centre*, Riverhead Books, New York, 2000.

Dilgo Khyentse, *The Wish-Fulfilling Jewel*, Shambhala, 2004 (first published 1999).

Nyanatikola, *Buddhist Dictionary*, Buddhist Publication Society, Kandy, Sri Lanka, 1997.

Rahula, Walpola, *What the Buddha Taught*, Grove Press, New York, 1974.

Salzberg, Sharon, *Loving Kindness*, Shambhala, Boston & London, 1995.

Other

Baring, Anne and Cashford, Jules, *The Myth of the Goddess: Evolution of an Image*, Viking Arkana, 1991.

Bartholomew, Alick, *Hidden Nature: The Startling Insights of Viktor Schauberger*, Floris Books, Edinburgh, 2003.

Bernays, Edward, *Propaganda*, Ig Publishing, New York, 2004 (first published 1928).

Brown, Lester R., *Eco-Economy*, W.W.Norton & Company, New York and London, 2001.

Cadman, David, *The Roots of Sustainability*, The Prince's Foundation for the Built Environment, 2009.

Cadman, David, *The King Who Lost His Memory*, www.davidcadman.net

Campbell, Joseph, *The Hero with a Thousand Faces*, Paladin, 1988.

The Gospel of Thomas, presented by Hugh McGregor Ross, Wilkins, 2003 (first published by William Sessions, 1987).

Lane, John, *Timeless Simplicity*, Green Books, 2001.

Lane, Robert E. *The Loss of Happiness in Market Democracies*, Yale University Press, 2000.

Leunig, Michael, *The Curly Pyjama Letters*, Viking Australia, 2001.

The Mabinogion, translated by Gwyn and Thomas Jones, Everyman, 1992.

Milne, Joseph, *Metaphysics and the Cosmic Order*, Temenos Academy, 2008.

Nassoudi, Mehrdad (editor), *The Value of Values*, University Press of Maryland, 2005.

Norberg-Hodge, Helena, *Ancient Futures: Learning from Ladakh*, Rider, London, revised edition, 2000 (first published 1992).

Perry, Whittall, N, *A Treasury of Traditional Wisdom: An Encyclopedia of Humankind's Spiritual Truth*, Fons Vitae, Louisville, KY, 2000. The new edition of this is now called *The Spiritual Ascent*.

Schauberger, Viktor, *The Schauberger Keys*, edited by Alick Bartholomew, see www.schauberger.co.uk

Shah, Idries, "The Initiation of Malik Dinar", *Tales of the Dervishes*, Octagon Press, 1982.

Sherrard, Philip, *Christianity: Lineaments of a Sacred Tradition*, T&T Clark, Edinburgh, and Holy Cross Orthodox Press, Brookline, MA, 1998.

Julian of Norwich: Revelations of Divine Love, translated by Clifton Wolters, Penguin Books, 1966.

Vailant, George E., "Positive Emotions, Spirituality and the Practice of Psychiatry", *Mens Sana Monographs*, Vol. 6(1), Jan–Dec 2008, 49.